For You

Andreas Seidl

Handover of Power

Global Version

Volume 21: Family

Imprint

Bibliographic information of the German National Library: The German National Library lists this publication in the German National Bibliography; detailed bibliographic data are available on the Internet at http://dnb.dnb.de.

© 2022 Dipl. Pol. Theodor Andreas Seidl

Cover: Christiane Ebrecht
Translation: DeepL, Cologne
Production and publishing: BoD – Books on Demand, Norderstedt

ISBN: 978-3-7568-0082-7

Acknowledgements

My thanks go to my family and friends who have made me who I am today. Special thanks to all those who supported me in writing this book. I would like to thank all my classmates, teachers, fellow students, lecturers, demonstrators, activists, colleagues, companies and countries with whom I have had the privilege of sharing the experiences from which all the ideas in this book have emerged. I would like to thank the staff of Books on Demand for their kind helpfulness. I thank the citizens of Seligenstadt for the harmony and solidarity in which I was able to write.

Foreword

This policy concept contains a variety of proposals for possible political reforms. It can be peacefully and democratically adapted to any current political system of any state in the world, but also to political systems in families, clubs, associations or companies. Wherever humans make or submit to rules that manage living together, the following proposals can be helpful. Readers who find the proposals so helpful that they would like to implement them together with like-minded people can contact the author. The contact form on the last page can be used for this purpose.

Faults and defects

I ask for your understanding that this volume was not professionally proofread. I could only afford professional proofreading for the summary. Spelling errors and unfortunate phrasing may therefore occur. As soon as this volume has sold enough to pay for a professional proofreading, it will be done. After that, a new edition will be published.

English version

Please understand that this volume has been translated automatically. I could only afford a professional translation for the summary. Poor wording and spelling errors may therefore occur. In case of doubt, the German version shall prevail. As soon as this volume has sold enough to pay for a professional translation, it will be done. After that, a new edition will be published. It was more important to me that no one in the world should have an information advantage than individual translation errors in the complete work.

References
If something has been quoted directly, it is set in italics. If the headings contain footnotes, the sources for direct and indirect quotations apply in the chapter for which the heading stands. Otherwise, quotations or source references are directly at the word or at the end of the sentence or paragraph. This book contains parts of text based on the Federal Constitution of the Swiss Confederation of 18 April 1999 (as of 12 February 2017), abbreviated to BV[1] and the Constitution of the Canton of Bern of 6 June 1993 (as of 11 March 2015), abbreviated to KV[2] .
If the constitutional paragraph, or individual paragraphs thereof, are based in whole or in part on extracts from the BV or KV, this is indicated in a footnote. The references to the corresponding footnotes for constitutional paragraphs are usually found after the heading of the affected chapter and sometimes in the body of the text. Articles used in the Swiss constitutions are listed in the footnote with a number after the title of the constitutional paragraph. Example: §123 Sample title: BV Art.123, KV Art.123.
All internet sources are fully cited in the footnotes. They were last accessed on 30.09.2021. All literature sources are also listed in full in the footnotes.
All references to tasks undertaken by other ministries and described in more detail there are given in footnotes. Example: Model Ministry - 1.2.3 Model Chapter.
All footnotes are to be viewed in comparison to the respective source, so-called indirect quotations. Direct quotations are set in italics, but hardly ever occur. The source reference is intended to enable further investigation and to take copyright

---

1 This is not an official publication. Only the publication by the Swiss Federal Chancellery is authoritative. https://www.fedlex.admin.ch/eli/cc/1999/404/de On 14.12.2021
2 This is not an official publication. The Bernese Official Collection of Laws is authoritative. https://www.belex.sites.be.ch/frontend/versions/2420?locale=de#ART71 On 16.12.2021

into account.

Table of contents

1 Goals of the Ministry of Family Affairs

The Ministry of Family Affairs aims to create a family atmosphere in the country in which humans are encouraged to love each other. To this end, the ministry offers advice and opportunities to find friends and partners for life as easily as possible. Through partnering, the Ministry of Family Affairs aims to create a parenthood that ensures an average of 2.1 children per woman with the lowest possible infant mortality rate. With this birth rate, the country is able to keep the population at the same level in order to avoid demographic fluctuations that can lead to crises in the labour market.

The aim is to make the age of the parents dependent on the partners' desire to have children and thus to enable a short or long succession of generations in equal measure. Children conceived out of love and growing up in the loving partnership of their parents is the ideal goal that the Ministry of Family Affairs strives for with its laws and measures. Parents should know how to give their child the best possible opportunities for its life and for this purpose they make the parenting licence. The aim of the Ministry of Family Affairs is to ensure the greatest possible freedom of love and at the same time the greatest possible security of voluntariness. Children are not forced to live with their parents and love them of their own free will. Living in a youth centre or children's home is possible at any time. Humans are not forced to live, but live because they love life. Suicide is possible at any time. Humans are not forced to love certain sexes or age groups, but choose their partners freely by mutual consent. The Registry Office certifies the voluntary nature and consent of the partners.

The Ministry of Family Affairs pursues the goal of providing assistance to the population in all private and personal situations, if they request it or if peaceful coexistence requires assistance or supervision. In accordance with the policy theory of the state as an entrepreneur of the national economy[1] , the Ministry of Family Affairs fulfils the human resources division of the company for employee recruitment and employee satisfaction. The family is the nest in which human capital

------

1 Ministry of State Organisation - 5.3 Theory of the state as an economic entrepreneur

regenerates, draws strength and reproduces. Children enjoy compulsory education and the right to a Tax-funded supply of knowledge and to be provided for entirely independently of their parents. Citizens of age are customers, employees and voters of their state as a company and are considered satisfied if they can obtain leisure time and care for recreation in addition to work.

The aim of the Ministry of Family Affairs is to enable free love in the country, which allows love for the fatherland and all fellow human beings. The people form a large family that speaks the same language. The municipalities are the small families that have the same living environment.

2 Departments

The departments are divided into sub-departments and enumerations are usually considered as their individual units. Many tasks of some departments are completely taken over by other ministries as a service.

2.1 Central Department

Part of the Central Department is the Reception Office with the Courier and Mail Room, which directs all concerns, broadcasts and visitors to the appropriate place in the ministry.

2.1.1 Staff

The Human Resources Department is responsible for staff development and planning. For this purpose, it takes care of the recruitment of junior staff, intern and trainee programmes as well as the selection procedures for employees and special selection procedures for applicants with disabilities. For politicians and employees, the department prepares a job plan. In all its tasks, it works in voting with the personnel board.[2]

All other personnel matters are transferred to the respective ministries. The Ministry of Education is responsible for the training and further education of employees for the

____

2Ministry of State Organisation - 2.1.1.1 Personnel board

state service.[3] The Ministry of Labour takes over the service law.[4] This includes the labour and collective bargaining law for employees in the state service, remuneration, personnel administration of all careers and employees, flexitime, holiday and sickness records, working time with or without flexitime in part-time or full-time at the place of work or in home work. The Ministry of Infrastructure provides housing assistance for all state employees.[5] The Ministry of Finance's Pay Office takes care of employees' salary, expenses, travel and relocation costs.[6]

The Ministry of Education provides childcare for all employees in the state service.[7]

The Ministry of Health is responsible for the occupational health service.[8] It ensures occupational health management, deals with the treatment, education and prevention of occupational accidents, controls and provides occupational health and safety through the health auditors[9] of the Company Auditing Agency[10].

2.1.2 Organisation

The ministries of media, security, justice, finance, labour, state organisation provide audit services for quality management in the ministry, evaluation of work performance, revenues and expenditures, as well as corruption prevention, sabotage protection and, if necessary, disciplinary matters.[11]

The Ministry of Labour regulates procurement law and ensures corruption-free state orders and procurement.[12] The

---

3 Ministry of Education - 2.1.1.1 Education and training for the state service
4 Ministry of Labour - 4 State enterprises, 13 Labour Directory
5 Ministry of Infrastructure - 2.1.1.1 Housing assistance for state service employees
6 Ministry of Finance - 2.1.1.1 Staff remuneration
7 Ministry of Education - 2.1.1.2 Childcare for state service employees
8 Ministry of Health - 2.1.1.1 Occupational Health Service
9 Ministry of Labour - 20.7.2 Health auditor
10 Ministry of Labor - 20 Company Auditing Agency
11 Ministries of Media, Security, Justice, Finance, State Organisation - 2.1.2.1 Audit services
12 Ministry of Labour - 6 Procurement Office

Ministry of Finance organises the annual budget vote and ensures proper accounting in each ministry.[13] It regulates budget procedures, budget law, staff budgets, departmental budgets, costs and cash management, and assists ministries in budget planning for the budget vote. The language service for translating talks or texts is provided by the Ministry of Education.[14]

The Ministry of Digital Affairs supports the supply of Information Technology.[15] In voting with the Procurement Office of the Ministry of Labour, it takes care of the procurement, provision, maintenance and service of technical devices and software. Much of this is produced in-house to ensure data protection in information and communication technology. Information technology and digitalisation officers audit and advise the ministries. Digital appointment calendar and documentation services are provided as well as a digital policy archive including a library.

2.2 Management Department

The Management Department is the minister's department. With his office team, he provides policy planning and analysis for his ministry and coordinates the relationship between the nation and the municipality through exchanges with his deputies in the municipalities. He initiates cooperation with other ministries or citizens in committees and is supported by the Ministry of State Organisation.

The Ministry of Media Affairs, through its media service, provides press and public relations for the ministry, moderates civil dialogue, trains or provides a spokesperson for the minister, writes speeches and texts on request, and ensures the implementation of conferences and events.[16]

The Ministry of Digital Affairs is responsible for digital management and thus provides departmental management. It automatically produces business statistics, staff surveys and

---

13Ministry of Finance - 8 state revenues, 9 state expenditure
14Ministry of Education - 2.1.3 Language Service
15Ministry of Digital Affairs - 2.1.2.1.1 Supply of Information Technology
16Ministry of Media Affairs - 2.2.1.1 Media Service

the current state of research through statistics. It automatically forwards proposals to the affected or empowered state employees. In document management, it ensures digitalisation and that ministries share forms with each other.[17]

2.3 Foreign Department

The Foreign Department oversees all matters of international family policy assigned to it by the Ministry of Foreign Affairs. This includes the adoption of foreign children, the immigration of foreigner families and their care by the Youth Welfare Office, whether all local obligations are complied with. The Foreign Department conducts continental and international youth policy. To this end, it establishes contact between continental or international youth organisations and the Youth Alliance and suggests exchange programmes between youth centres. The same applies to the Seniors' Alliance and old people's homes in the course of international policy for senior citizens. Continental and international gender equality policy is pursued in cooperation with the Ministry of Foreign Affairs, which aims to harmonise the requirements for gender equality within the International Union[18] and to agree on international requirements on the basis of human rights. The Foreign Department is responsible for international sports matters when it comes to organising international championships and Olympiads abroad.

2.4 Family Department

The Family Department ensures cooperation with other ministries to uphold the principles of manners and democratisation. It oversees the work of the Registry Office and improves life support and cure of souls services in cooperation with the registrars. It runs the Institute for Family Research in cooperation with the Ministry of Education. It ensures participation in studies and a forwarding of data to

---

17Ministry of Digital Affairs - 2.1.2.1 Digital Service
18Ministry of Foreign Affairs - 5.8 International Union

the responsible authorities of the Ministry of Family Affairs. It operates the Family Directory[19] in cooperation with the Ministry of Digital Affairs. In cooperation with the Minister of Family Affairs, it drafts laws and model forms for partnering and marriage and forwards them to the Registry Office once they have been enacted.

2.5 Children's Department

The Children's Department prepares the templates for laws on childbearing in cooperation with the Minister of Family Affairs. For this purpose, it organises cooperation with the ministries of health, labour and economy. It supervises the Youth Welfare Office. In cooperation with the Minister of Family Affairs and the appropriate specialists of the Ministry of Education, it compiles the contents of the parenting licence and coordinates the allocation of premises. In cooperation with the Minister of Family Affairs, it prepares draft legislation on children's rights and forwards amendments to the Youth Welfare Office. The requirements for the child ID card are developed with the Ministry of Integration and changes are communicated. The same applies to child benefits with the Ministry of Finance and to the Youth Alliance with the Ministry of Security.

2.6 Senior's Department

The Senior's Department looks after institutions for recreation, senior citizens and death. It checks whether the offer of art, music, sports, playgrounds, old people's homes and cemeteries is sufficient. If no one else wants to provide the facilities, the Senior's Department takes the lead in ensuring that they are accessible to all age groups. It runs the Club Directory and organises cooperation between clubs, honorary services and state institutions. In cooperation with the Ministry of Health and its gene database, the department operates the ancestral archive on the intranet. Together with the Minister of Family

---

19Ministry of Digital - 12 Directories

Affairs, the Senior's Department draws up legal requirements on death, suicide, inheritance and burial, as well as a model template for wills. It ensures the proper operation of the suicide cells.

3 Tasks of the Ministry of Family Affairs

The Ministry of Family Affairs is responsible for ensuring that the population lives together in a family-like, peaceful and democratic manner. In order to ensure peaceful coexistence, the Ministry of Family Affairs issues laws on manners, which describe personal and communal moral responsibility in handling one another.

In order to ensure democratic coexistence, the Ministry of Family Affairs enacts laws to measure and promote democratisation in the population and equality and democratisation of all subsystems for minors. The Youth Welfare Office oversees democratic coexistence in institutions that work with children.

The Ministry of Family Affairs has a family policy for parents, children, youths, unmated persons and senior citizens. The Registry Office and the Youth Welfare Office work with the population to implement the family policy. The Family Directory and the Club Directory enable citizens to communicate with each other and with the state in order to organise family life digitally.

The task of the Ministry of Family Affairs is to prescribe a legal arrangement for the best interests of the child, marriage and inheritance, to which citizens can or must adhere in part. Parents draw up guidelines on how to promote the best interests of the child, married couples conclude a marriage contract and deceased persons have a testament. Citizens are advised by the Registry Office and Youth Welfare Office on their path through life and, if necessary, supervised at times.

The Ministry of Family Affairs is responsible for guaranteeing family coexistence for all nationals and all minors. To this end, it works with the ministries of education, infrastructure and Planned Economy, as well as with clubs, youth centres and old people's homes.

Last but not least, it is the task of the Ministry of Family

Affairs to ensure cultural coexistence. This includes the legal definition and the promotion of music, art and sport through training and application events.

The Ministry of Family Affairs becomes increasingly important as automation and Unconditional Basic Income[20] increase and the population turns away from work towards family and leisure. In the long term, an earlier birth of the first child can be assumed and a shortening of the generation sequence. It is the task of the Ministry of Family Affairs to accompany this transition, especially in the youth centres, and to inform the Statistical Office[21] of these demographic changes at an early stage.

4 Manners[22]

The Ministry of Family Affairs defines the good manners that distinguish moral from immoral behaviour. They are derived directly from the constitution and are to be taken into account in legislation as well as in jurisprudence. Each person is responsible for himself, humanity and the environment.

4.1 Personal responsibility

Personal responsibility lies in owning one's own life and being the owner of one's own body. Every human being is allowed to do anything with his or her body and mind, as long as he or she does not damage any other human, animal, plant or ecosystem and complies with applicable law. The Ministry of Health determines when animals, plants and the ecosystem are harmed. The ministries determine in their penal laws when damage is done to a human being. Whether a human is not harmed in an individual case is determined by the treaty between the humans who cause the damage and those who suffer it. It must be clear in the contract that the human wants to suffer the damage, that the originator wants to cause the damage, that both bear any costs of the damage and how the creation of costs for bystanders or the environment is

20 Ministry of Finance - 6 Unconditional Basic Income
21 Ministry of Digital Affairs - 6 Statistical Office
22 §5 Individual and social responsibility: BV Art.6, §6 Moral obligations

excluded. The treaty must be examined and deposited in the Registry Office before it becomes valid. The examination is carried out by the registrars, who can have the treaty checked by the Company Auditing Agency's health auditors to ensure that there is no cost to the public. Other humans are harmed as soon as they report the damage and can justify it with the constitution or laws. They are supported in this by the police and the courts. Other persons are not harmed if they are merely disturbed by the behaviour because it does not correspond to their own, but do not suffer any personal damage. In that case, the principle is "live and let live." Another principle is: "Ignorance does not protect against sentence." Therefore, it is considered inadmissible to commit a crime and claim one was not aware of the crime. It is up to the human to inquire about the rules of his environment before testing them. Exploiting the ignorance of other humans consciously to one's own advantage or their disadvantage also does not protect from a sentence. Because humans must ask each other for permission before they are allowed to harm each other, such ignorance cannot exist.

4.2 Social responsibility

Personal freedom and security ends where the freedom and security of another person begins, because humans are there to make each other happy and not to harm each other. This makes it necessary for humans to vote on their ideas of freedom and security, which is the task of the state. Since all nationals are part of the state, they take responsibility for their people within the national borders. In the long run, national borders disappear and peoples merge into one people, which is responsible towards humanity.
All humans are equal because they belong to one species and can all produce fertile offspring together, regardless of which race they belong to. The protection and preservation of the human species is the goal of humanity and belongs to the life task of every human being. Humans have this task in life in common with all living beings on earth. As the only living being on earth with the privilege of the most intelligent

consciousness, humanity also has the duty to save the living beings of the earth from extinction through the destruction of the earth. Exceptions of species must be decided by majority voting, such as mosquitoes or pathogens. In order to protect humans and the environment, states adopt requirements and measures. In case of doubt as to which end justifies which means, the principle applies that special situations require special measures. Laws serve to describe the situations and measures as precisely as possible and to determine short-term and short-lived measures for unforeseeable situations without a legal basis. The Ministry of State Organisation regulates this state of exception.[23] Families and companies can use it as a guideline if they experience a personal or company state of exception.

As a state community, the nationals set themselves rules on how to protect and preserve the environment for their descendants. These tasks must be fulfilled in such a way that the will of the majority is fulfilled and suitable niches are created for minorities. In case of doubt as to which tasks are to be fulfilled and how, the use of the most useful and majority idea always applies, whether in the state or in society. The goal should be that unjustly acting humans have as little influence as possible on rightly acting humans. For example, children should be able to play alone in the forest and not be forbidden to do so only because there are child molesters. If there is such a danger, the state has failed because it is making bad policies. Instead of resigning in fear, the people have the duty to empower the state powers.[24]

5 Promotion of democracy

The Ministry of Family Affairs is responsible for the promotion of democracy among the population. Its approach is to ensure that children grow up in a democratic environment. This approach follows the principle of subsidiarity and federalism, so that adults only have responsibility over a child until it is able to assess the limits and consequences of its own actions. In negotiations with adults, children should learn where

23 Ministry of State Organisation - 12.6 State of exception
24 Ministry of State Organisation - 12.3 Popular empowerment

humans come up against legal or natural limits that must be observed in order to avoid a sentence by humans or nature. Legal boundaries are reflected in rules for living together and are basically negotiable by humans. The principle applies that the will of the majority counts and the will of the minority is taken into account through rules of exception.

The Youth Welfare Office is the supervisory authority responsible for ensuring the democratisation of all subsystems in all institutions where adults interact with children. It conducts surveys and research on voter turnout and the employment situation of women and men, old and young. The results show where there is a need for support and where there is sufficient democratisation and equality.

A sufficient degree of democratisation is achieved if every citizen has taken an interest in at least 2 ministries, has participated in a committee[25] at least 2 times in 10 years and has taken part in voting at least 2 times within 5 years. Citizens who fall below these thresholds are investigated to see if they have lent out their voting rights to party delegates. All citizens who have not done so and are below the thresholds are the target group to which the democratisation measures will be tailored. It is possible to invite the affected citizens to the Registry Office for a voluntary consultation.

5.1 Equality

Sufficient equality is achieved when women, men, young and old have the same opportunities. The Ministry of Family Affairs monitors equal opportunities and can set requirements for other ministries to bring about equality through law. Particular attention is paid to sector-specific employment situations of women and men, old and young, which is dominated by one of these groups. Care must be taken to ensure that the disproportionate presence of one group is due to differences in lifestyle and not to coercion or exclusion. For example, posts for politicians cannot be allocated according to quotas for one group. Since entrance to a party is free, no group is disadvantaged. Who runs for election as a party

---

25 Ministry of State Organisation - 9.6 Committee

member is also open to everyone. For example, a quota can be given for teachers because the choice of teachers in an educational institution is limited and children meet different needs through the choice of caregiver.

5.2 Democratisation of all subsystems

The Ministry of Family Affairs, together with the Ministry of Education, ensures that all subsystems that care for and educate children are fully democratised. Teachers and educators as teachers in educational institutions should not be authoritarian rulers. Their task is to exemplify democratic coexistence and to provide all the necessary means for this. The subsystems in educational institutions are the courses whose content and division of tasks are determined by the teachers and students in free, fair and equal elections.

Teachers ensure that children live together peacefully and explain what emotional and physical injuries cause in other humans. Teachers justify all sentences pronounced. As long as a child ensures the freedom and integrity of his fellow human beings through his actions, he is not to be punished. Teachers are mediators of knowledge for peaceful and democratic coexistence. Otherwise, it is their task to provide an eventful and eventful environment in which a child can discover the parts of the world that interest him or her.

Teachers ensure that children have admission to all necessary areas of knowledge. The areas of knowledge needed are defined in the curriculum, which is democratically negotiated.[26] In accordance with the principle of subsidiarity, only a learner himself knows how he learns best so that he understands the knowledge and can use it for as long as possible. Therefore, the compilation of the timetable and the selection of the teacher is up to the learner and is similar to the election of persons process.[27]

Teachers are allowed to choose their own style and method of education, just as politicians are allowed to choose their own programmes. For all rules of regularisation, there are

---

[26] Ministry of Education - 4.4.2 Curriculum development
[27] Ministry of State Organisation - 9.9 Elections of persons

assemblies in which an equal number of children and adults are involved and entitled to vote.[28]

6 Registry Office[29]

The Registry Office consists of all the registry offices in the town halls and the central office in the ministry's capital city. It is responsible for the execution of civil status. It is largely guided by the Civil Status Act.[30]

The Registry Office is responsible for issuing birth certificates, marriage certificates and death certificates and accompanies the affected persons and their relatives before and after the respective event in their lives. It forwards the collected data of all issued certificates to the Ministry of Digital Affairs in order to record the state and development of the population as accurately as possible.[31] The data from all Registry Offices is used to determine the birth rate, divorce rate, death rate and suicide rate.

The Registry Office, like any agency, may be administered municipally, i.e. administer local laws at the municipal level with the consent of the population, provided they do not violate the constitution.

The laws on birth, marriage and inheritance apply equally to nationals and foreigners. There is no entitlement to traditional, ethnic or religious difference for birth, marriage and inheritance. The applicable requirements already contain sufficient leeway for personal arrangement.

6.1 Life support

Before the birth, parents are educated about the coming care and parenting of a child through the parenting licence. After the birth, parents must state the name and gender of their child and receive the birth certificate in which the parenting licence passed is noted. With the birth certificate, parents must then

---

28 Ministry of Education - 5.10 Rights for learners
29 §11 Right to marriage and family: BV Art.14, §188,1,6 Statistics: BV Art. 65
30 https://www.gesetze-im-internet.de/pstg/inhalts_bersicht.html
31 Ministry of Digital Affairs - 6 Statistical Office

have a child ID card issued for their child at the Residents' Registration Office. The Youth Welfare Office is responsible for the child and the family. With the age of majority, persons can change their name and gender at the Registry Office.

Before marriage, citizens are supported in finding a partner through appropriate events. After partnering, voluntary partners receive advice on relationship problems. Business partners can also make use of this counselling service. Persons of any gender and any number of persons can marry each other to become spouses. The marriage must be performed by a registrar, who verifies that all participants decide to do so voluntarily. He or she informs the spouses of their future rights and obligations towards each other. The registrar asks each person wishing to marry individually and alone whether he or she wants to marry of their own free will. For this purpose, each partner must fill out a form alone at the Registry Office in the presence of the registrar. If the marriage is not free, the coerced person can immediately go into hiding in a Social Village and the coercing person receives a charge of coercion. Rights and obligations are regulated in a marriage contract, which is sealed by the registrar and attached to the marriage certificate. The marriage contract is required by law and can be changed by the spouses as long as all spouses agree to it.

If there is a divorce, the Registry Office is responsible again. It advises the spouses before the divorce on how relationship problems could be solved so that the divorce does not have to take place. In the event of divorce, the marriage certificate is confiscated and its contents become null and void. While at least two persons are required for marriage, only one person is required for divorce. If more than two participants are involved in the marriage, the marriage can continue between the other persons, even if one person divorces. The Registry Office monitors compliance with the marriage contract with regard to agreements in the event of a divorce and settles minor disputes. As soon as the spouses cannot come to an amicable agreement, the case is heard in court.

Before death, the Registry Office advises persons on how they wish to regularise their estate and write their will. The testament is prescribed by law and can be changed by any person at their discretion. The original of the current testament must be deposited at the Registry Office.

If a citizen wishes to commit suicide, he or she must declare in a counselling interview at the Registry Office, in particular that he or she chooses to do so voluntarily and is not forced or coerced by anyone. In addition, he receives suitable therapeutic or social offers of help, which he may or may not accept.

After the death, the Registry Office looks after the surviving dependants by issuing the death certificate, opening the will and supervising its observance. The issuing of the death certificate and the opening of the will only take place once the People's Computer[32] of the deceased has been handed in. The Registry Office settles disputes and refers the case to the court if the participants cannot come to an amicable agreement. It advises relatives on suitable forms of burial and assistance facilities for coping with grief and provides cure of souls in acute cases.

In the event of death, the People's Computer is confiscated by the Registry Office. Its data is stored in the ancestral archive so that the ancestors can research the biographies. The device is formatted and re-issued.

6.2 Cure of souls

The Ministry of Family Affairs maintains a pastoral care centre in its capital city. There, trained cure of souls attend to concerned citizens of all ages by telephone and digitally. The telephone counselling service can be reached from the domestic telephone number 0049. The intranet chaplaincy can be reached via the profile page of the Ministry of Family Affairs. It offers assistance and help with psychological or social problems. On the phone or in personal news, concerns are discussed and responsible agencies are proposed, such as psychologists, Youth Welfare Office, Registry Office, People's Protection Service or the Social Village. At the request of the person concerned, the responsible office is notified.

Honorary service volunteers are citizens who report wanting to be involved in the cure of souls. They can choose duty

32Ministry of Digital Affairs - 13.6 People's Computers

periods when they will be involved in telephone and digital cure of souls from their homes.

7 Families[33]

The Ministry of Family Affairs is responsible for measures to protect the family and to create conditions through which families can meet their needs. The needs of a family are personal closeness, attention to each other, caring, understanding of each other, procreation and parenting. In a narrow sense, families consist of parents and their children. How many parents of which sex have children, or vice versa, plays no role. In a broader sense, it also includes more distant relatives, neighbours and friends. The family is the place where a human is socialised. Children learn there how humans interact with each other as a group who have become familiar with each other over a long period of time.

The Ministry of Family Affairs protects the family in the narrower and broader sense with its measures. Measures to protect the family can be implemented by the Ministry of Family Affairs or the implementation of private organisations or persons is supported. Support is provided through the Family Directory, where, for example, the organisation providing rest for stressed mothers offers cures for parents and children.

To help citizens start a family, events and dating databases are offered. The Registry Office offers advice on relationship problems. As soon as children live in a family, the Youth Welfare Office provides additional support with its services for advice, training and accommodation. In order to strengthen the family's parenting skills, parents must take a parenting licence, which teaches them about the age-related characteristics of children and ways to handle them without conflict.

To facilitate family life in the country, family-related services are reviewed for completeness and effectiveness. The decisive factor for effectiveness is the well-being of families. The Institute for Family Research conducts the measurements in cooperation with the Company Auditing Agency via surveys.

33§11 Right to marriage and family: BV Art.14, §234,1 Children's rights, child benefit and parental protection: BV Art. 116

The yardstick for successful family life in the country is a birth rate around 2 children per woman, a low divorce rate and suicide rate. The Ministry of Family Affairs monitors births and ensures that the necessary skilled workers are recruited or trained for the respective ages of the children born. In particular, it instructs the Ministry of Education to ensure that there are sufficient places in educational institutions. In cooperation with the Ministry of Labour, a family-friendly working environment is created that enables parents to spend sufficient time with their children. In cooperation with the Ministry of Infrastructure, attention will be paid to a family-friendly infrastructure that favours the use of prams and gives young humans as many opportunities as possible to participate in society.

7.1 Institute for Family Research

The Institute for Family Research is the scientific advisory board of the Ministry of Family Affairs and its authorities. It researches which events or circumstances are capable of disrupting or unifying family relationships. It evaluates data from the directories and maintains research communities with state personnel involved in parenting. Its research targets the causes and effects of rising and falling rates of births, marriages, divorces, suicides and unmated persons. On the basis of happy or unhappy individual fates, requirements or measures are developed that enable more humans to have a happy fate. Requirements are, for example, laws on the welfare of children that prohibit certain forms of behaviour towards children. Measures are, for example, therapy options for individuals or families.
Another part of the research deals with family models and their effects on family members, especially children. It examines how the personal development of adolescents is influenced by heterosexual, homosexual, monogamous and polygamous forms of relationships in their family.
Based on the results of the Institute for Family Research, the Minister for Family Affairs can propose laws and measures. The citizens vote on the laws and the financing of the measures.

7.2 Family Directory

The Family Directory offers family members a platform to exchange information. Each family receives a profile and all profiles from the Persons Directory who follow the profile are family members. All those who are friends with the family profile are friends of family members. Persons of the same age form reference groups in which they give each other advice on how to cope with similar life situations. Reference groups exist for mothers, fathers, parents, grandmothers, grandfathers, grandparents, disabled persons and their relatives as well as same-aged single children, older, middle and younger siblings, girls, boys, couples and unmated persons.

In the Family Directory there are also profiles for outpatient family assistance agencies, youth centres, Youth Welfare Offices and Registry Offices. These profiles are imported for state institutions from the State Directory[34] , where authorities have their groups. Companies import their profiles from the Labour Directory[35] and associations import their profiles from the Club Directory.

In addition to the usual tools for creating posts, comments, replies and voting, the Family Directory offers even more useful tools. These include tools for meeting, settling disputes, finding friends and partners.

7.2.1 Meeting

In order to meet, one has to select those with whom one would like to meet. To do this, users select the persons they want to meet if they know them. If they are looking for people similar to these persons, users create one or more avatars that have all the desired characteristics, such as age, gender, abilities, opinions or interests. Users have the option to search for similar or opposite characteristics to their personal ones or those of another selected person. The search is done by an algorithm so that not every user has access to all data sets in order to personally make all comparisons. A radius search

---

34 Ministry of State Organisation - 4.5 State Directory
35 Ministry of Labour - 13 Labour Directory

can be used to display all persons to whom the data apply. The prerequisite is that the persons concerned have given their consent to be displayed and contacted anonymously. To meet, an appointment planner and a map of the surroundings can be used to arrange the meeting place.

Peers can form a group with which they can book a staging area to meet regularly. Staging areas are, for example, at the local youth centre, on state-owned land or in state-owned buildings that are unused at the time.

7.2.2 Settle disputes

A facilitation tool can be used to settle a dispute. Everyone involved in the dispute should be alone in a room with their People's Computer, if possible. All participants can use the tool at the same time or with a time delay. Each person personally decides which form suits them best. Persons who wish to use simultaneous dispute resolution can do so. The persons who prefer to use time-shifting provide their input either before or after simultaneous dispute resolution. Each participant describes how they currently feel when they think about the dispute, then what the factual basis of the dispute is, what their relationship is to the disputant(s) and what demand they have of the disputant(s) to end the dispute. All participants look at the contributions of the other participants involved. Then questions of understanding can be asked. In the last step, one or more solutions are agreed upon, for which the Solution Finder procedure[36] can be used. If a participant still wants revenge and is not satisfied with the solution alone, virtual court proceedings can be held to determine a sentence and penalty. The procedure is similar to that of the education court.[37] The participants are family members and friends of the family who are involved in the necessary elections and voting. A family dispute without a criminal offence cannot be tried in a state court. A family dispute with a criminal offence

---

36Ministry of Media Affairs - 7.2.3.5 Solution Finder (Legislation Committee)
37Ministry of Education - 5.10.7 Education court

must be heard in a state court.[38]

7.2.3 Make friends

To find friends, a user can import their friends list from the Persons Directory[39] or use the search function for meetings. Users also receive references to the Club Directory, which unification might match their interests or which members of a unification have the characteristics of the avatars described.

7.2.4 Partner exchange

To find a partner, each user has to fill out a questionnaire and create two avatars. One avatar corresponds exactly to the user and contains all data from all directories. The second avatar corresponds as closely as possible to the partner they are looking for. The questionnaire asks about life goals, life attitudes, sexual likes and dislikes and exclusion conditions. All identified interests, likes and dislikes that have been imported from other directories about oneself are queried for their matchability.
An algorithm automatically calculates the matching partners and displays them in a list. The list can be sorted by closest match or proximity. Users can select further sorting options from a keyword list, such as age, educational qualification, number of siblings or similar. The profile of a potential partner can be viewed via a link to the Persons Directory and contact can be made with him or her via the messaging service. Users of the partner exchange can expand their profile from the Persons Directory for users of the partner exchange. They can post their own pictures, videos and sound recordings which are not visible to Persons Directory users. In order to meet each other, users can use the tool to meet. Anyone who has found a partner must log off from the partner exchange. Those who are looking for a partner again after a break-up can retrieve their details from the previous registration and

---

38 Ministry of Justice - 5.4 Courts
39 Ministry of State Organisation - 4.6 Persons Directory

change them or create new ones altogether. If only sex is being searched for, this must be indicated on the profile page in the partner exchange so that other users can filter their search results according to this characteristic.

7.2.5 Adoption database

In order to adopt a child, persons who declare their willingness to adopt and have been classified as suitable by the Youth Welfare Office receive a profile. In order to be adopted, children who would like to be adopted and have reported this to the Youth Welfare Office receive a profile.

The profile corresponds to the profile from the Persons Directory if it is a single person. If it is a couple or a family, their profile from the Family Directory is used. Additional information can be provided, pictures, videos and sound recordings can be uploaded. Based on the matching information, suitable persons are proposed to each other, similar to the tool for finding friends or the partner exchange.

7.2.6 Parenting licence portal

All persons doing a parenting licence use this tool. It is structured like the Education Directory[40] , but only the learning parents and teaching trainers and their training locations are listed. Participants in the Parenting Licence receive all information and lists for seminar dates in all state educational institutions in their postcode area and can upload performance records. Parents with a parenting licence who have current questions about the parenting of their children can also get help here. They can select and attend suitable ongoing courses here so that they can be discussed there as case studies. They can also post their questions on the noticeboard.

---

[40] Ministry of Education - 5.9 Education Directory

7.3 Partnering[41]

The Ministry of Family Affairs is responsible for the promotion of sexuality, partnership and gender as well as the reduction of taboos in this context. It issues the following requirements on sexual education and permissiveness, which are taught in educational institutions and observed in public, state institutions and companies.

The sexual instinct is part of the human being from birth and only has something criminal about it when it damages other humans. The Ministry of Family Affairs, in voting with the people, is developing identifying signs and phrases that humans can use to ask each other whether or not they want to mate. Ambiguous allusions, which can degenerate into coercion and uncertainty, are thus to be avoided. There is no compulsion to use it, but it can be requested from the other person in order to clearly express willingness or unwillingness to partnering and thus avoid a criminal offence of harassment or rape. If you want to be sure, always ask first. If you want to be absolutely sure, obtain written or digital consent, which you can also have notarised by the Registry Office.

Partnering includes partnered love, which includes sex, or coming together for sexual purposes without love. Love is defined as regular caring, caressing and kissing. Sex is the arousal of the sexual organs or sexual intercourse.

A human who wants to mate must announce or indicate to his or her counterpart whether he or she is seeking sex or love. Sexual or loving acts may only take place when the other person has consented. The request and consent can be given orally, as a show of hands, in writing or digitally. The written consent puts the oral consent formulas in writing and must be accompanied by the signature, name, birthday and place of birth of all participants. After mutual consent, all participants are considered to be partnered. Partnering requires at least two humans, their gender or other characteristics are irrelevant. Exceptions apply in the case of minors.

---

41 §7.4 Personal rights

7.3.1 Digital consent

Digital consent is the safest form of partnering to exclude rape. It can be given either by the participants themselves with their People's Computers, or by registrars.

Digital consent is obtained by partnering in the Family Directory by creating a profile that all participants follow. Those who create the profile with a People's Computer must then scan all the identity cards of the participants involved into their People's Computer so that they follow the profile. Civil registrars who certify a partnering always create a profile and mark it "certified" on the profile page. Changes are then only possible in the Registry Office.

In the profile, the participants describe as precisely as possible the love relationship or sexual relationship that is being lived. Especially if violence or coercion are to be part of the relationship, possible risks to the health of those affected must be named. As long as all participants are aware of the risks and no bystanders are harmed, everything is permissible. Digital consent thus becomes a personal expression of sexual self-determination. The more precisely it is described, the more legally secure the partnering becomes. The profile can be continuously adjusted by all participants involved with mutual consent. If it is certified, the adjustments must be made by a registrar or all participants declare to the registrar that they wish to withdraw the certification.

7.3.2 Love

Those who aspire to love can say: "I have fallen in love with you." or show half a heart as a hand sign. The other person is then obliged to answer either: "Me too" or "Not me". As an affirmative hand signal, show half a heart. This hand signal is already known as a heart. To do this, you take both hands, curl the fingers slightly, the thumbs point stretched downwards, touch at the tips of the thumbs and the fingers touch at the opposite fingernails. The new hand sign is simply one hand of it, i.e. the right or left. As soon as the other person repeats this hand signal, regardless of which hand, the heart is complete and getting to know each other is desired. A negative sign is a shake of the head or a fist with the thumb or index finger stretched downwards.

Love is a feeling that comes over humans when they experience another human and feel attracted to him or her. It is not yet known why this feeling cannot be managed and why it arises suddenly in some humans and gradually in others. It is crucial that potential partners tell each other whether the feeling of being in love has come on suddenly or gradually. If necessary, the other person needs more time for the feeling to set in or can rule it out. Both are to be announced. Which statistical peculiarities and personal characteristics could further fathom this phenomenon of sudden or insidious infatuation is the subject of research by the Institute for Family Research.

As soon as a human is overcome by the feeling of love, he or she is considered to be in love. If this feeling also comes over the other person, both humans are considered to be in love with each other and are in a love relationship. The love relationship is considered confirmed as soon as the partners give their consent to it. As soon as the feeling of love solidifies, does not fade away even after weeks and becomes familiarity, the partners love each other. As soon as the feeling of love fades for at least one partner, the love relationship is considered to have ended. The one for whom love has passed must tell the other, "I no longer love you". The love relationship can then be resumed as soon as both give their consent again. The unilateral imposition of love, although objected to by the other person affected, is considered harassment and is punishable by law.

7.3.3 Sex

A person seeking sex can say: "I want to have sex with you." or point to the person in question as a hand signal with an outstretched thumb and index finger. The other person is then obliged to answer either: "Me too." or "Not me.". An affirmative hand signal is to point at the person with the same sign. This sign is already known as a pistol, where the thumb is folded in while pointing. A sign of disapproval is a shake of the head or a fist with the thumb or index finger extended downwards.

Sex is a feeling that comes over humans when they experience another human and feel sexually aroused by him or her. Sexual arousal makes itself felt through a sudden activation of the sexual organs. The stimuli that are sexually arousing in men or women have been largely researched by sex research and the sex industry. The Institute for Family Research examines the results and confirms or refutes them in experiments. Sex usually involves French kissing, orgasms with the sexual partners, or putting over or penetrating the body of the sexual partners with the help of the sexual organs or objects. The possibilities are manifold and should therefore be agreed upon by all participants involved or refrained from in case of refusal. If no contraceptives are used, which must be announced before sex, sex serves to fertilise the egg cell by a sperm cell in the course of sexual intercourse, thus creating humans. Due to the release of happiness hormones, sex has an intoxicating effect on all participants if there is mutual consent and preferences are taken into account.

As soon as a human is overcome by the feeling of sexual arousal, he is considered horny. If this feeling also overcomes the other person, both humans are considered horny for each other and are in a sexual relationship. As soon as at least one partner is no longer horny, he or she must indicate this to the other person with the words: "I don't want to have sex with you any more. This ends the sexual relationship. It can be resumed as soon as both partners newly give their consent. Unilateral forcing of sex is considered rape and is punishable by law.

Sex as a trade is permissible. Anyone who is engaged in the sexual trade must explicitly declare this at the time of contact and keep a company in the Labour Directory. Prostitution is possible in all four economic forms. The relevant occupational safety and occupational health regulations of the Ministry of Health apply and are regularly reviewed by the Company Auditing Agency's health auditors.[42]

---

42 Ministry of Health - 4.5.5 Institute of Occupational Health, 4.4 Company Auditing Agency health auditor

7.3.4 Minors

Partnering is only possible without restrictions from the age of majority. In the case of minors, unconscious sexual development is assumed until the age of 10, and only after this age is conscious partnering possible, because by then sexual education at school has already taken place. In general, an age difference of no more than 3 years applies to partnering between and with minors. In the case of requests, the refusal must be justified with the age information. In voting on partnering and requirements for minors, the votes of 10 to 18 year olds are counted separately because they are affected citizens.[43] No majority decision can be taken against their will. The right to sexual self-determination is lifelong.

7.3.4.1 Unconscious partnering

Until the age of 10, love and sexual relationships are considered unconscious developmental events that are mostly experienced playfully. An age difference of no more than 3 years is to be observed. Children's sexuality is to be regarded as natural and allowed as long as none of the participants expresses their aversion verbally or by turning away, crying, crying or rejecting gestures. If aversion is expressed and not heeded, the duty of supervision and immediate protection of the affected child takes effect as long as the child has not already freed itself from the situation or is unable to do so. The necessarily interfering of supervisors in the child's sexuality must be explained to the originator and affected child. The originator child should learn to understand how to react to expressions of aversion with disinterest instead of intrusiveness. The affected child should learn to understand how to express his or her aversion as clearly as possible and to move away and seek supervision if the intrusiveness does not subside.

In the case of consciously acting adults who deal with unconsciously acting children, or parents of these children, it can come to loving or sexual acts on the part of the children towards the adults. At the beginning of life, children's sexuality

---

43 Ministry of State Organisation - 8.1.2 Affected citizens

develops unconsciously, or rather in an undirected way, and is directed towards their fellow human beings. At this stage of development, children are unable to make a clear distinction between affection, kindness, love or sex.

Adults should explain to the child the separation between affection, kindness, love and sex as soon as a situation requires it. They should not punish the child's loving or sexual acts, but ask the child to stop the acts with them and to leave or withdraw. If the child asks, they can refer to this law. In case of repeated occurrences or doubts in the rating of unconscious partnering, affected persons can have a counselling talk with them and the child at the paediatrician or Youth Welfare Office.

7.3.4.2 Conscious partnering

As soon as minors are able to give their consent consciously and to assess the consequences, they may mate with each other. The age difference between the minors must not exceed 3 years. If minors wish to enter into a partnership, at least one parent can request recognition by the Registry Office.

If minors and adults want to partner with each other, the age difference must not exceed 3 years and the partnering must first be recognised by the Registry Office and checked for voluntary on both sides before the first sexual or loving acts. In addition, it must be in written and digital form.

7.3.5 Groups

If love or sex as a corporate or private act takes place alternately between many persons, all individual persons must declare their consent with each other. General consent may be obtained in writing and must be entered in the Family Directory via the People's Computer or by scanning the identity card as partnering. If the consent is revoked or the agreed room is left or the agreed period has expired, the partnering is again considered cancelled.

7.3.6 Punishable acts

Sexual harassment occurs when a human repeatedly asks another human for sex or love, even though the affected person has already refused to have sex or love. Anyone who uses sexual stimuli in a targeted manner to sexually arouse a human being, but has refused to have sex with him or her, can be reported for sexual harassment by the repeatedly affected counterpart who cannot avoid it. Sexual harassment does not exist if the arousing stimuli are used to sexually arouse a human with whom one would like to have sex, even if this sexually arouses other humans with whom one would not like to have sex.
Rape is when sex or love is performed against the will of the affected counterpart.

7.3.7 Events

The Registry Office encourages partnering through partner search events. The events are partly organised by the Registry Office on its own, partly in cooperation with the Ministry of Media Affairs, or as voluntary requirements at corporate or private events. Events run by the Registry Office with the Ministry of Media Affairs are the shows "Flirtwalk" or "SOS Singles on Stage".[44] Some of these events are broadcast on Youth Television[45] , the others are not recorded or broadcast. Get-to-know-you events held at parties or after stage events are the "Half Heart" events and the party game "Who was single?".

7.3.7.1 Sign of the hand "Half Heart"

At events with a stage, at least 5 unmated persons should be allowed to go on stage at the end and introduce themselves for about 30 seconds. In the crowd, those who would like to meet the person then raise their hands with the hand sign "half

---

44 Ministry of Media Affairs - 14.3.4.2 Flirtwalk, 14.3.4.3 SOS Singles On Stage
45 Ministry of Media - 14 Youth Television

heart". Each unmated person who has introduced themselves can create a profile in the Family Directory, which can be followed by anyone in the audience who has held up a half heart. The place, date and time of the event and introduction must be entered in the profile so that the search engine can display the matching persons.

7.3.7.2 Party game "Who was solo?"

When entering a party, newcomers are asked if they are unmated persons and want to be mated. Anyone who wants to is given a sticker with a number and told to put it on their left breast. On a noticeboard, the number is written and whether one is looking for love or sex. Shy people can give their phone number if they don't want to be approached directly. The winner is the first and last couple to leave the party.

7.4 Marriage

Marriage is a special form of partnering entered into through marriage. The marriage is performed in the Registry Office and is based on mutual consent of all spouses in addition to the rules on certified partnering. Any number of persons of each sex may become spouses. Marriage includes a love relationship and a sexual relationship, but can also last without love or sex. Marriage regulates in particular the name, mutual support, division or separation of jointly used goods, as well as the distribution of inheritance and child custody for own and adopted children. Marriage serves in particular to procreate, care for, parent and support children who arise between and live with spouses. This is intended to create a regulated and thus more stable family environment for adolescents until they reach the age of majority. Parents do not have the obligation to marry, children do not have the obligation to live with their parents. Spouses can get divorced if at least one spouse wants to do so. The divorce is executed in the Registry Office and accompanied by the Youth Welfare Office if there are children from this marriage. Only if spouses cannot agree on matters that were not settled in the marriage contract will their case be heard by the Municipal Court.

7.4.1 Marriage contract

When marrying in the Registry Office, a marriage contract must be concluded by all spouses. The compulsory portions contained therein can be changed by the spouses by mutual agreement. If they cannot agree, the terms of the marriage contract determined by law apply. The Ministry of Family Affairs issues an individually extendable standard contract in voting with the Ministry of Justice. The prenuptial agreement must cover all areas most frequently litigated by courts when spouses dispute names, property, assets, maintenance, child custody or inheritance after divorce. The purpose of the mandatory prenuptial agreement is to avoid post-separation disputes, in particular their effects on the children, the courts, the administration or survivors.
The headings of the standard contract are the compulsory parts that every marriage contract must contain as a minimum and on which the spouses must provide their own details if they wish to amend the statutory standards.

7.4.2 Marriage name

The spouses agree on a surname that at least one of the spouses already bears. After a divorce, the spouse who had taken the surname of the spouse must change his or her surname. He or she is given back the surname he or she had before the marriage. Children of married parents receive the married name as their surname. Illegitimate children can decide on a surname of one of the parents and bear a double name consisting of the surnames of the parents until their decision is made.

7.4.3 Goods

Matrimonial property law governs the matrimonial property regime of partners who are married. As a standard model, married couples inland form a community of acquisitions. This means that any assets that existed before the marriage remain with the respective persons. Any assets that come into existence during the marriage belong equally to the spouses. If there is a divorce, the assets that were created during the marriage are divided equally between the spouses. In the event of death, 50% of the assets go to the heirs and 50% to the remaining spouse(s).

The registrars inform the spouses about the possible matrimonial property regimes before the marriage. If the spouses share their assets, this is considered community of property. In the event of divorce or death, the assets are divided as above. If the spouses separate their assets, this is considered separation of property. In the case of separation of property, the assets are not divided in the event of divorce and are inherited in the will of the owner in the event of death.

The community of joint ownership corresponds to the community of joint acquisitions, but the assets that existed before the marriage are included in the assets that come into existence during the marriage.

The community of accrued gains corresponds to the community of acquired property, but the assets of the spouses remain separate. Only in the event of divorce are the assets created during the marriage divided equally between the spouses.

Gifts do not have to be reimbursed in the event of divorce, regardless of whether they were made before or during the marriage.

7.4.4 Pension rights adjustment

During marriage, the spouses and their children are insured as a family. Who pays the contribution is irrelevant. As soon as the spouses marry, the entitlements to benefits, So-called entitlements, are transferred to the joint assets. This applies to state insurances, especially insurances for pension, care, occupational disability or life insurance. Private insurance companies can negotiate their own conditions in the treaties with their policyholders. In the event of divorce, there is a separation of property and the entitlements acquired during the marriage are divided equally between the spouses and their children. The entitlements acquired before the marriage remain with the respective spouse. In the event of death, the entitlements shall pass to the remaining spouse(s) and children, unless otherwise specified in the testament of the deceased.

7.4.5 Post-marital child support

In the event of divorce, there is only a claim to post-marital maintenance if children have arisen from the marriage and child custody has not been divided equally between the spouses. The person who has a lower share of child custody is obliged to pay maintenance on a pro rata basis. For example, someone who takes care of their child 49% of the time must pay 2% child support. With 2%, it is 96% accordingly. If siblings are divided equally between both parents, the right to child support does not apply. For example, a husband and wife have three children. One is 100% with the father, one 50% with father and mother and one 100% with the mother. There is no entitlement to child support for illegitimate children.
The amount of child support is based on income. The maximum amount per child is 20% of the income. From the third child onwards, the 60% of the income is divided equally among all the children. When marrying, the spouses must disclose how many children they have been obliged to pay maintenance for up to now. The amount of income is recorded via the business tax. Employers are obliged to report to the Registry Office on a monthly basis the remuneration paid to employees who are obliged to pay maintenance. Child support is transferred monthly to the children's account .[46]

46Ministry of Finance - 11.5.5 Children's account

7.4.6 Child custody distribution

Parents are granted shared child custody of the children they have fathered together, whether they are married or not. The division of child custody and the expenditure of time and money is 50% for one parent and 50% for the other.
In case of separation, parents are obliged to present their children at the Registry Office within 2 weeks. In the case of divorce, parents must go to the Registry Office to get divorced. Child custody is also distributed there.
Children are informed about their rights regarding the division of custody at the Registry Office. They have the right to obtain a different division of child custody at the Registry Office as soon as they can express themselves linguistically and independently. An employee of the Youth Welfare Office must be present at the distribution of child custody. He advises the registrar and ensures that the best interests of the child are respected. At the time of the statement, no relative or relative may be present who could be biased in any way.
Children can choose the parent they want to live with fully or partially. If they wish to live partially with one parent, they must indicate a number of days per month, which is converted into a percentage that takes into account all days of the year. Each child decides individually which of their parents' child custody arrangements applies to them. For example, a child may decide to live 20% with the mother and 80% with the father, while his sibling wants to live 100% with the mother. Separation of siblings is possible as soon as a sibling decides to do so.
The registrar hears all affected parties individually and records their wishes about the distribution of custody. If the wishes are contradictory, the registrar conducts a counselling interview with all participants involved and tries to find a compromise. If no compromise is reached, the children decide alone. If no agreement is reached even then, the parents must have the court decide on a distribution.

7.4.7 Distribution of inheritance

After their death, the spouses leave an equal share of their inheritance to their spouse or spouses and, if applicable, to their children. In the event of divorce, divorced spouses have no claim to the inheritance and drop out of the succession. Children from this marriage remain in the succession. Changes can be stipulated in the marriage contract, in the testament or in an inheritance contract.

7.5 Desire to have children

After partnering, sexual acts are possible that can lead to the conception of a child. Anyone who does not want this to happen must tell the other person and all participants must avoid it by using contraceptives. Should an unwanted pregnancy nevertheless occur, the woman has the right to have a medical abortion, which she pays for herself. She has the right to claim half of the costs from the partner with whom she conceived a child despite contraceptives. If sexual intercourse took place without contraceptives, cost sharing is only permissible if the desire to have a child was denied by all participants before the sexual intercourse. If the sexual partners do not agree on the desire to have a child, but have conflicting wishes, sexual intercourse must be refrained from. Those who wish to have a child can fulfil it with a partner, a surrogate mother, sperm donation, egg donation or adoption. After partnering, mutual consent must be obtained and sex must be performed without contraceptives. If the ability to procreate or give birth is not possible for one of the participants for medical reasons, all medical interventions that can restore this ability are permitted.[47] Exceptions apply to interventions that the people have rejected by a majority after an ethics committee and a committee.[48]

---

47 Ministry of Health - 5.4.2.2 Reproduction
48 Ministry of State Organisation - 8.5.9 Ethics Committee, 9.6 Committee

7.5.1 Procedure in case of inability to conceive

If the woman is unable to give birth, an egg can be removed from her and artificially fertilised with a sperm from the man she has chosen and who has agreed to, or a sperm donation from the sperm bank. The fertilised egg can be transferred to a surrogate mother. If the woman has no fertile eggs, her genetic material can be removed and inserted into the egg of a surrogate mother and artificially fertilised with a sperm. If possible, the woman can also carry this artificially fertilised egg to term herself if she is medically able to do so. Otherwise, she must use a surrogate mother. A surrogate mother is not entitled to child custody. She can refuse to disclose her identity to the child, but she does not have to. Egg donation is also possible for implantation by a surrogate mother or a woman with an unfulfilled desire to have a child.

If the man is unable to conceive, a sperm cell from the sperm bank can be artificially inseminated with the egg cell of the woman he has chosen and who has agreed to, and implanted in the woman. Similarly, the genetic material of the man who is inability to conceive can be inserted into the sperm cell from a sperm donation. The use of a surrogate mother and a donated egg cell is also permitted.

Specialised urologists and gynaecologists are responsible for medical interventions. For male homosexuals, surrogacy, sperm and egg donation is possible, whereby they can also inseminate a voluntary woman themselves with their sperm after her consent. The use of a surrogate mother and artificial insemination is not mandatory. For female homosexuals, the use of a sperm bank is possible, whereby they can also be inseminated themselves by a voluntary man after his consent with his sperm. The use of sperm donation and artificial insemination is not mandatory.

Surrogate mothers, egg and sperm donors are listed in a database to which the attending physician has access. The data of their profiles from the Persons Directory are displayed there, but without name and address. Physicians ask their patients what their preferences are and narrow down the search accordingly. Patients can view all search results and select the most suitable. Patients can also do without this selection step and randomly choose a sperm donor or a surrogate mother.

Those who want to fulfil their wish to have a child through adoption should contact the Youth Welfare Office.

7.5.2 Pregnancy

The use of any drugs, such as cigarettes, caffeine, alcohol or marijuana, is prohibited for women during pregnancy and breastfeeding. For men, this prohibition applies three months before conception because sperm cells need that long to mature. If a violation is reported by citizens to the police or observed by authorities, blood, hair and urine samples are taken from all parents. In the case of sperm donors, a urine sample is required before sperm donation, and in the case of surrogate mothers, before fertilisation or implantation. For fathers and mothers, samples are taken after a reported suspicion, as soon as a physician has determined the pregnancy.

If the offence can be proven, the mother is taken into custody in the family home of a Social Village. For men, an imprisonment of 3 months follows. In the case of the mother taken into care, possible drug use is constantly controlled by urine samples in the hospital of the Social Village. If drug use is proven despite being taken into care, detention follows for the duration of the pregnancy and breastfeeding.

7.5.3 Birth[49]

As soon as a physician determines the pregnancy, he or she enters this in the Health Card of the pregnant woman. The Ministry of Health reports this data to the Ministry of Family Affairs, which then contacts the parents-to-be. An invitation is sent with suggested dates for birth preparation courses and registration for seminars for the compulsory parenting licence. Within the first 3 months of life, newborns are visited monthly by field workers from the Youth Welfare Office. They advise parents on which bureaucratic steps are necessary and help

---

49 §234.4 Children's rights, child benefits and parental protection. KV Art.41

them fill out the necessary forms. Parents can ask questions or seek further help with parenting or care. During the first visit, the Youth Welfare Office staff create the profile for the newborn in the Persons Directory and record all the necessary data to create an identity card. They report the data to the Residents' Registration Office and the Registry Office. The Registry Office produces the birth certificate, the Residents' Registration Office the identity card.

7.5.4 Parental leave[50]

The Ministry of Family Affairs regulates parental leave in voting with the Ministries of Health, Labour and Economic Affairs. Parental leave is so that parents can be with their newborns. Mothers are granted sick leave for 4 weeks after the birth. A father and mother who have given birth to a child have the right to take 12 months of unpaid leave each from the birth of that child and then continue to be employed. Parental leave must be taken within the first 30 months of the newborn's life. How the father and mother divide the parental leave is decided by them in voting with each other and their employers or co-workers. However, parents retain the final decision-making right. In particular, parents are free to spend 12 months together with their newborn, alternate for a total of 24 months, or find some intermediate solution. Once both parents are working again, they can place their child in a nursery school .[51]

Parents can build up their own savings for this time or join the parental insurance scheme[52] to receive 80% of their previous monthly income each month during parental leave.

In order to be able to spend time with their own children beyond parental leave, parents can also work in partner work[53] . If they do not both have the necessary qualifications for this, one parent must undergo further training in order to fill the position in partner work. The prerequisite is that the revenues

50§234,4,5 Children's rights, child benefit and parental protection: KV Art.41, BV Art. 117a
51Ministry of Education - 7 nursery school
52Ministry of Social Market Economy - 17.5.2 Parental Insurance
53Ministry of Labour - 16.4 Partner work

from the one job that is filled in partner work are sufficient to support the household.

From their eighth child onwards, parents are offered by the Youth Welfare Office the opportunity to alternate between further training as educators and opening a voluntary nursery school ([54]). If the family owns a house, they can use this house as business premises. If they do not own a house, the Youth Welfare Office provides the necessary premises in cooperation with the ministries of education and infrastructure. The parents receive additional educators depending on the size of the institution. For every 20 children, one additional educator is provided by the Ministry of Education.

Parents can also decide that one parent is a housewife or househusband and takes care of the parenting of the children and the household instead of being gainfully employed. If parents are in a marriage without separation of property, the one who takes care of the children and refrains from gainful employment receives 50% of the spouse's income and, if applicable, makes his or her contributions for pension insurance from this.

7.6 Youth Welfare Office[55]

The Ministry of Family Affairs operates the Youth Welfare Office to ensure the best interests of minors in the country. The Youth Welfare Office consists of all branches in the town halls. It is responsible for inspecting the institutions where children are present and persons who work with children before they start work and regularly during operation. The verification takes place announced, unannounced or covertly in cooperation with the legality auditors[56] of the Company Auditing Agency. Checks are made to ensure that children and youths remain mentally and physically unharmed and that their development is age-appropriate. Parents are only examined at the beginning of parenting and thereafter only

---

54 Ministry of Education - 7.5 Voluntary nursery school
55 §8,1 Protection of children and youths: BV Art.11, §179,2,3,4
Promotion of children and youths: BV Art.67
56 Ministry of Labour - 20.7.6 Legality auditor

if there are indications of a risk to the welfare of the child. At the beginning of parenting, the parenting licence must have been passed before the birth of the first child. Parents can contact the Youth Welfare Office with questions about parenting, problems in the relationship, marriage, sibling relationship, attendance at a care or educational institution. There is an ombudsman for children, mothers and fathers at the Youth Welfare Office in every town hall. A mediation appointment can be arranged here at any time. There, those affected receive initial counselling and contact addresses for training in educational institutions, relationship counselling in the Registry Office or offers of help from providers of non-state youth welfare.

In addition to the educational institutions' parenting work, the Youth Welfare Office also offers events in which children, youths, parents and families receive targeted support. Events for children are holiday camps, for youths regular festivals, for parents discussion groups and for families exchange programmes. All participants are put together by the Youth Welfare Office in such a way that they come from similar milieus, but in the families there are sometimes perfect and sometimes problematic circumstances. Through the exchange, both sides can learn from each other. A stay in the upbringing camp or special school can be ordered by educational institutions, courts or the Youth Welfare Office, with the following consequences for parents.[57]

7.6.1 Duty of supervision of paediatricians

All paediatricians are in constant contact with the Youth Welfare Office. They have the right to file a suspicion report with the police if they believe the child is being beaten or traumatised. This is followed by covert surveillance or unannounced checks by the civil police and arrest if the suspicion is confirmed. Paediatricians may order a more balanced diet or a sports club. If this has not been implemented by the next doctor's visit, a report is made to the Youth Welfare Office. This is followed by sentences for bad parents. Paediatricians can send

---

57 Ministry of Education - 5.17.7 Upbringing camp, 6 Special school

observation forms for children of concern to teachers via the Youth Welfare Office.

For minors, visits to the paediatrician are compulsory until the age of majority. The older one gets, the less frequent are the compulsory examinations and vaccinations. Religious, traditional, cultural or ethnic reservations by parents are not permitted.

7.6.2 Behaviour in the event of a risk to the welfare of a child[58]

All state employees and paediatricians who can regularly observe children are released from their duty of confidentiality towards the Youth Welfare Office if there is a suspected case of child welfare endangerment. If a child has bad grades, has difficulty making friends, comes to the educational institution hungry or dirty, or becomes violent towards himself or other humans, the Youth Welfare Office is called in. The teacher is the first person to visit the family. She must at least be shown the children's room. The teachers and paediatricians have a contact person at the Youth Welfare Office who accompanies them on the visits if they request it. If there is a suspicion that a child's well-being is at risk, a report must be filed with the police, who will initiate all further proceedings.[59]

7.6.3 Family assistance

The Youth Welfare Office organises family assistance for individual family members or the whole family in cooperation with the local Social Village. This benefit is available to all minors and nationals of age of majority. Children can live in the children's home. Parents can receive help with parenting at the children's home. This ranges from short counselling sessions with the pedagogical staff of the Children's House to outpatient day care and permanent accommodation. Inpatient family assistance can be called upon immediately

---

58§179.2 Promotion of children and youths
59Ministry of Justice - 8.4.4 Child welfare endangerment

when children become orphans or parents become widows or widowers, or when citizens of any age are fleeing their families. Separated parents move with their children into the house for single parents, single separated parents into the house for unmated persons. If a whole family is to be cared for, they move to the House for Families in the Social Village. There, they receive daily visits and assistance from social workers of the Children's House as well as practical exercises and further training in the Education Centre.[60]

7.6.4 Sentences for bad parents

Bad parents are those who do a poor job of parenting, caring or nurturing their child and thus endanger the child's well-being. For teachers and paediatricians, the following signs are considered crucial.

If a teacher sees that a child hits frequently, is constantly abusive, steals from other children or is generally in a neglected state, i.e. poor clothing, nutrition or communication skills, she notifies the Youth Welfare Office. As an immediate measure, the Youth Welfare Office sends a family counsellor. He visits the family twice a week for a period of 3 months and has a catalogue of measures that he may order. The measures correspond to an exemplary relationship with the child, with which the child's well-being is best promoted according to current scientific knowledge. For example, the use of digital devices may be prohibited and playing with parents in nature may be ordered.

If measures ordered are violated or suspected of being violated, the penalties listed below will apply.

If a paediatrician discovers wounds that could be the result of abuse, he or she orders the keeping of a wound book and informs the Youth Welfare Office of the order. During follow-up examinations, the wounds and symptoms are checked. If the symptoms then do not match the entry in the wound book, the sentences listed below kick in.

---

60 Ministry of Planned Economy - 18.1.7 Children's House, 12.3.8 House of Families, 12.3.6 House of Single Parents, 12.3.5 House of Unmated Persons, 18.1.8 Education Centre

Depending on the frequency and severity of the violations against the best interests of the child, a higher sentence is imposed by the Youth Welfare Office. Those affected can appeal against penalties imposed by the Youth Welfare Office to the local court, thus opening up legal recourse.

In the first stage, a parenting course is arranged. Parenting courses are available at the parenting licence offices in the town hall and at each local primary school on weekday evenings, alternating with the parenting licence courses. If parents do not attend the parenting course as instructed, a monetary fine is due each week. The monetary fine is less for lateness or failure to complete tasks than for absence.

The second stage is used if the parents do not manage to deal better with their child despite the course. Then each family member has to see a psychologist with outpatient sessions until a diagnosis is made for each family member. This is followed by family therapy. The regulation of psychoactive medicines is not allowed in the second stage.

In the third stage, the parents have to participate in the upbringing camp[61] for one week. Their children live in the children's house during this time. In the upbringing camp, the parents spend a week in a state boarding school where there is only sleeping, studying, eating and sports. The atmosphere is like that of basic training for those doing military service. The curriculum of the parenting licence applies, with increased content on the stages of development and a root cause analysis of the parents' childhood and their child's childhood to date. The aim is to identify omissions and poorly mastered developmental stages and to make up for them.

In the fourth stage, the children have to move to the children's home and attend the special school while their parents are liable to detention for 3 months.

In the fifth stage, the child is placed in psychiatric care. This order must be made by a court. The court decides which parent must remain in detention for as long as the child must remain in psychiatric care. The court can withdraw child custody from one or both parents for a limited or unlimited period of time. The children are taken into state custody in

____

61 Ministry of Education - 5.17.7 Upbringing camps

the children's home or given up for adoption if the children so wish.

7.6.5 Adoption

Unwanted children can be handed in by their parents at any Social Village. There they are placed in the children's home and entered into the adoption database of the Family Directory. Children can also make this decision themselves if they have spent at least 12 months in the Children's Home on their own initiative and ask the Youth Welfare Office to be released for adoption. Children can make this decision up to 3 times during their minority, i.e. to move into a foster family, to their own parents or to the children's home. Potential foster parents and children can get to know each other in the Social Village before the adoption. Only if the adoptive parents, their children as well as the children who are given up for adoption agree, the adoption will be carried out. Children who cannot yet speak are familiarised with their possible foster parents according to the familiarisation model[62] of crèches. If they accept them as caregivers, the adoption is carried out. Adoptive children have the right to know who their birth parents are and to contact them at any time. The Youth Welfare Office is responsible for arranging contact and accompanies the adopted children as they get to know each other, if they so wish. Every year, foster children have to present themselves at the Youth Welfare Office and the child is interviewed individually to see if he or she is doing well.

7.7 Parenting

Parenting means supporting adolescents in their development into mature humans who are faithful to the constitution. This includes imparting the domestic culture with its virtues and values. Parenting is limited to persons who are parents or who are not yet of age of majority. The citizens are called upon

---

62Laewen, Hans-Joachim, Andres, Beate, Hédervári, Éva: Die ersten Tage - ein Modell zur Einewöhnung in Krippe und Tagespflege. Cornelsen Verlag Scriptor 7th edition 2011 ISBN 978-3-589-24730-1

to report observed misbehaviour directly to the parents and/ or children and to state why this should be misbehaviour. Educational assistance by the social environment is considered civil courage. The aim of the Ministry of Family Affairs is for the population to have the courage and pride for a high level of moral courage. This human quality is crucial for the functioning of a direct democracy. In this way, moral courage ensures parenting towards becoming a responsible citizen.

Targeted parenting by the Ministry of Family Affairs takes the form of the parenting licence, and children are taught by teachers in educational institutions how to live with parents, children and other citizens. Educational institutions and youth centres look after minors away from their parents' homes. Youth Welfare Offices supervise age-appropriate parenting and care in educational and care institutions for minors. In addition, there are punitive measures for parents and children imposed by the Youth Welfare Office or the ministries of security and justice. Families are monitored as soon as paediatricians or staff of education and care institutions suspect a risk to the welfare of the child.

7.7.1 Parenting licence[63]

With the parenting licence, the Ministry of Family Affairs offers children sufficient protection against a risk to child welfare due to ignorance on the part of the parents. Just as drivers are trained in the operation of a motor vehicle in road traffic, parents are trained in the parenting of a child for a low-conflict and non-punitive coexistence in society. During the lessons, parents are given advice on child-appropriate parenting and care from pregnancy to the age of majority. The lessons are divided into theoretical and practical learning phases. The final examination consists of a theoretical and practical test, which can be passed or failed. Examinations that have not been passed can be repeated as often as desired. The Youth Welfare Office is responsible for cooperation with parents and educational institutions. It accepts registrations from parents and takes the examinations. The occupancy of

---

63 §179.3 Promotion of children and youths

rooms in the educational institutions is coordinated with the Ministry of Education and teachers are organised for lessons. Classes are held in the local nursery schools, primary schools and comprehensive schools. The lessons on the different developmental stages of the child are held in the educational institution that suits the respective developmental stage.

For expectant parents, the child benefit applies from the time the pregnancy is diagnosed by a physician, which covers the expenses for the parenting licence for both parents without co-payment.

After the birth, the parenting licence must be shown to the physician who assisted at the birth. The same applies when applying for a birth certificate at the Registry Office and for admission to a nursery school or school. If there is no parenting licence, the responsible workers must send a report to the Youth Welfare Office, inform the police and refuse to provide services. Physicians are exempt from refusing service. If only one parent has the parenting licence, that parent gets sole child custody until the other parent also has a parenting licence. As long as neither parent has passed the parenting licence, the child does not get a birth certificate and the family has to move into the Social Village. If parents refuse, the police will arrange for the move. Children with parents without a parenting licence attend day care in the children's house and live with their parents in the house of families. [64]

Parents who have once passed the parenting licence are from then on familiar with the laws on the welfare of children[65] . Persons who violate their duty of care towards a child act intentionally from then on. The parenting licence only has to be newly acquired if the best interests of the child have been violated and a court has ordered a sentence.

64Ministry of Planned Economy - 18.1.7 Children's House, 12.3.8 House of Families
65Ministry of Justice - 8.4.4 Child welfare endangerment

7.7.1.1 Registration

The parenting licence must be obtained before the first child. Anyone can register for it at the Youth Welfare Office at any time. Parents who are pregnant always have priority for enrolment. As soon as the pregnancy is established by the physician, he asks whether both parents already have a parenting licence. If not, he hands them an information sheet about the parenting licence and reports the pregnancy to the Youth Welfare Office.

Mother and father must go to the Youth Welfare Office and register for seminars during pregnancy at the latest. Seminar registrations are also possible via the Family Directory. The seminars take place in the evenings at local educational institutions. Dates and frequencies depend on the reported need from the Youth Welfare Offices. When registering, parents can indicate which dates would suit them best. The offers range from weekly appointments to block seminars at weekends. Depending on how many parents are registered, different appointment forms or the simultaneous offer of several courses are offered.

7.7.1.2 Contents

Parents learn in class what permanent damage is triggered in a child by taking drugs before or during pregnancy, hitting it, shouting at it during the first two years of its life or arguing in front of it. They also learn what good memories are left in the child when you stroke it, cuddle it, crawl it or kiss it, go on journeys with it to discover the environment, calmly explain to it what is happening to it at the moment or address everyday human needs such as tiredness, hunger, pain and being alone.

7.7.1.2.1 Case studies

Parents may attend the appropriate classes at any time if they are currently having problems with their child in the respective age group or developmental stage. The schedules and locations for the lessons of the parenting licence are available via the Family Directory. If possible, parents should register in advance via the Family Directory so that the teacher can include the case study appropriately in the lesson.

Parents who have passed the parenting licence are asked if they would be willing to come to class with their child in future training units to act out example scenarios from their lives. Those who agree will be invited to the appropriate lesson.

7.7.1.2.2 The most crucial time of life

Parents should realise that the first two years of life are crucial for a human's entire life. No one can remember these years of their life because the brain has only learned to remember during these years. If more bad things happen than good things during this time, memories are more likely to be recalled badly or badly, because that is how one has learned about the world. In the first two years of life, the subconscious is formed, which accompanies the human for the rest of his or her life. It is similar to a pair of glasses through which the world looks slightly different for everyone. Humans who have experienced too much bad things during this time then wear a darker lens and the world looks darker to them. Ignorance permanently damages the human's ability to bond for the rest of his or her life. No activity that the child executes is meant maliciously by him, because the child does not yet know what it is. Rules and boundaries are important, but they must be explained. Indulgence is paramount and unconditional affection, tenderness and care with food, talk, caresses, music, play, rest and sleep.

For parents it means that sometimes you have to act in front of the child. Peace, joy and harmony in partnership, family, living and working situations are paramount during these two years. Parents who have problems with this can set up a day a week when they can say or do anything and the child is looked after elsewhere. Thus, it is possible for all parents to take their child to a nursery school once a week during the first two years of life, so that they can argue at home in peace.

Little disputes, like "Where did you put that? Why didn't

you do what we agreed?" The child can and should witness this. In front of the child, however, it is essential to express the feelings that are hidden behind the facial expressions and gestures. In front of the child, you have to speak more openly about yourself, because in the end it is crucial how and why you act. Expectations and disappointments must be clearly expressed. Just as you explain plants to a toddler while holding him in your arms, you explain how you behave towards humans while acting together with other humans. The child observes everything and takes it in almost unfiltered. The filter in the brain for "What is example? What is serious, what is fun or even irony?" is only being built up in this phase of brain development. So in this phase of life, increased attentiveness is called for, which is exhausting, but the reward of these laborious two years pays off for the rest of life. The child becomes more good-natured and causes less noise, quarrels, hecticness, gluttony or offences.

7.7.1.2.3 Speak

Both parents take turns speaking the "DaDa language" to each other. First, one partner tries to say something with his mouth closed. The other partner just keeps saying "Da Da". No doubt this is funny, but no interaction can take place. Especially for children who cannot yet speak for themselves, all actions on and around the child should be announced by the caregivers. The parent pairs now practise this with each other in the play. From the colour of the stocking to the condition of the car door, simple information that fits the situation should be communicated to the child. This is the first science of being human, which every adult person masters, even if they cannot yet read or write. We all know what things are called and what can be done with them when we see or feel them. Babies can't know that yet. Parents should learn to use the time when their child cannot yet speak to build up a broad vocabulary and expertise in their child. Later on, the child will thank them with understanding and acceptance of rules that can be explained in an understandable way.

7.7.1.2.4 Dispute

Two parents are asked to act out an argument to the rest of the class as deputies for the child. In it, they reveal their feelings as clearly as possible. At the end there is either a reconciliation or one of them leaves the room. After the play, the group has to recount who acted how and why. Afterwards, the two parents who were on stage say whether what the group said was true, i.e. whether cause and effect matched and whether the feelings matched the behaviour. The teacher points out improvements and omissions. Each pair of parents has to act out each play once themselves, so that parents can learn what effect an argument has on the observer and how much of the content of the argument can be correctly understood.

7.7.1.2.5 Winding

All parents are to demonstrate the correct diapering process with a doll. Different situations are given by the teachers. Sometimes the child is tired before diapering, sometimes hungry. Afterwards, the parents take turns changing each other. For participants who do not want to be exposed, overclothes are put on. The parent playing the child should act out different situations, from stiffening of the limbs to fast frantic movements to crying and screaming. The swaddling parent should learn how to react calmly and carefully to unforeseen difficult situations.

7.7.1.2.6 Sign language

Parents are taught a basic vocabulary of sign language. This consists of, for example, "Yes, no, why, I'm fine, I'm not fine, I'm hungry, I need to go to the toilet, I have pain there...". Everything a toddler wants to say but cannot yet speak is included in the vocabulary. Parents learn to speak orally and simultaneously with gestures in front of and to their child. This means for all words for which they know the gestures, they make the gestures while speaking the word. The child thus learns the gestures and can respond with the gesture.

Signs require fewer and visible muscle movements and can therefore be performed months earlier by the child. This saves parents from uncertainty and children from feeling powerless.

7.7.1.2.7 Crawl

It means crawling with the fingers between tickling and scratching, as if a fly were walking on the skin. Especially on the back, it strengthens the productive capacity of the nervous system. Children learn to feel their bodies more quickly, the nerve pathways are trained and the sensorimotor memory is honed. Parents crawl each other in class and learn from the teachers where the nerve pathways run and how they should crawl them.

7.7.1.2.8 Discover body

For children, different parts of the body become increasingly important at different stages of life. Parents learn how these body parts function and practise it in a play as they would explain it to their children. The play is repeated for several years of life. The human speech apparatus is explained to toddlers, the digestive system to kindergarten children, the musculoskeletal system to primary school children, the sexual organs including sex education and the use of contraceptives to pubescents, as well as the stimulus-response pattern in the brain of youths. Parents should learn which information about their own body is important and how to help their children understand how it works and when. Especially during puberty, children consciously experience their bodily changes, and they should support their parents by providing explanations.

7.7.1.3 Foreigners

For foreigners, there is a lesson adapted to their country of origin, held in a place with enough equally affected foreigners. Foreigners learn about the differences in parenting between the inland and the other country. They learn that inland children are brought up with and through charity on the part of the parents. They receive background information about the religious worldview that has shaped the legal situation here. Simply letting children grow up, as can be the case elsewhere, is more likely to be the child's undoing in this country because the other children are not brought up in this way. Foreigners who wish to move inland with their children must pass the parenting licence within the first 9 months of their stay. Otherwise, the residence permit for the entire family will be revoked.

7.7.1.4 Seminars

The seminars take place in the educational institutions outside opening hours. Depending on which age is currently the subject of the lessons, the seminars take place in the nursery school, the primary school or the comprehensive school. The staff of the respective educational institution teaches the parents. On suitable dates, the lessons are held by midwives, doctors, psychologists, educationalists, social psychologists and sociologists. They explain the handling and nature of an infant, child and youths within their developmental stages and do a developmental stage test[66] of all developmental stages with the parents. Through practical examples, situations are acted out with the parents that can be everyday or extraordinary. During the lessons, practical tests are taken at the end of a lesson. The practical exams are considered performance records and are completed through acting out or simulations in virtual reality.[67] The examination scenarios are different each time and always involve a possible violation of the child's welfare. Any examinee who reacts incorrectly and endangers the child's welfare is made aware of this and must state how he or she would have behaved better instead. The re-examination takes place at the end of all practical courses.

---

66 Ministry of Education - 5.11.1 Developmental Stages Test
67 Ministry of Digital Affairs - 13.6.9.1 Virtual reality glasses

7.7.1.5 Exam

To obtain the parenting licence, the final exams must be passed. Attendance of the lessons is only compulsory if the final exams have not been passed once. As all lessons can also be accessed via the Knowledge Directory, parents can also learn the knowledge for the final exams through self-study.

Parents have the right to register for the exam at any time, compulsory hours are not necessary. The theoretical questionnaires are freely available as well as many practical positive and negative example simulations for each age range.

7.7.1.5.1 Final exam

There is a theoretical and a practical final examination. Both exams may be repeated as often as desired. The theoretical examination consists of a catalogue of questions that must be answered in a test and a guideline that must be written as a final paper.

The questionnaire includes questions about situations that could put parents in prison or children in state custody. For example, parents are supposed to know what they would lose their children for inland or what they would have to go to prison for themselves because they are liable for them. The test is conducted in classrooms. If the test is not passed 3 times, the lessons have to be attended in a non-digital seminar.

The final paper is also your own handbook for your time as a parent. All given contents should be summarised in your own words and sorted by years of life. This final paper is written by the parents at home, corrected by social education teachers from the state colleges and returned as pass or fail. Parents read their final papers to each other to align their parenting styles. Final papers in which more than 30% had to be corrected are considered failed. The final paper must be newly written and sent in for correction. If it is again deficient, the affected theoretical teaching content must be attended in non-digital seminars.

The practical test is a simulated situation from each of the age groups under three years, three to ten years and ten to eighteen years. This situation is simulated with Virtual Reality glasses[68] and headphones for the examinees, but is recorded once with real children. To simulate the handling, there are dolls in original child size in the classroom.

8 Children

The Ministry of Family Affairs protects children by formulating children's rights that must be observed by persons in their handling of children. In cooperation with the Ministry of Integration, children receive a child ID card and in cooperation with the Ministry of Finance, child benefits.

8.1 Children's rights[69]

The Ministry of Family Affairs is responsible for formulating the rights of the child. This describes the best interests of the child, which more precisely describes when children remain mentally and physically intact and how they are supported in their development in a manner appropriate to their age. Support includes the circumstances provided to children by their parents, self-selected caregivers, teachers in educational institutions or the Youth Welfare Office.

The Youth Welfare Office is also responsible for ensuring that the rights of children are respected by adults in their handling of children. It can take measures to accompany or restrict the handling of children. Employees of the Youth Welfare Office, in cooperation with auditors from the Company Auditing Agency, audit the companies and state institutions that work with children. Parents are trained in their implementation of children's rights through the parenting licence. Children are regularly informed about their rights by Youth Welfare Office staff and teachers in educational institutions. Education takes place whenever children are mentally capable of doing so or as soon as they are given further rights and duties from an approaching age. Youth Welfare Office staff educate children

---

68Ministry of Digital Affairs - 13.6.9.1 Virtual reality glasses
69§8,1,2 Protection of children and youths: BV Art.11, §179,2
Promotion of children and youths, §234,2 Children's rights, child benefits and parental protection: BV Art. 116

in their second and fifth year of life, if they are not already attending an educational institution by then.

Parents are monitored by the Youth Welfare Office as soon as children or adults express indications of poor implementation of children's rights to the Youth Welfare Office, physicians or the police. The Youth Welfare Office can take measures to avert a risk to the child's well-being in voting with the affected child. These measures range from family assistance and state custody of the child to detention of the parents or guardians. The Youth Welfare Office is entitled to propose offers of voluntary assistance to parents and adults dealing with an affected child. If coercive measures are to be taken which restrict parents or guardians in their right to custody, duty of supervision or right to determine residence, the Youth Welfare Office must first obtain a court order, check that it has been properly executed and report any violations to the responsible judge. The legal process is open to those affected.

Children's rights are granted to all children living inland, whether they are conceived in or out of wedlock, are domestic or foreign citizens, or are orphans. The only full obligation for children is compulsory education.[70] Children's rights specifically include the rights to relationships, rules, integrity, community, talent, experiences and future. Anyone who violates these rights commits child endangerment and is liable to prosecution.[71]

8.1.1 Relationships

Children have the right to consistent and loving relationships with at least 2 adult persons. These persons have the duty to accept the child as he or she is in order to develop a basis of trust as empathetically and caringly as possible. In this way, children should learn to build empathy and trust. Children have the right to decide in voting with the Youth Welfare Office whether they want to grow up in the care of their parents, the state or a foster family.

---

70 Ministry of Education - 5.4 Compulsory education
71 Ministry of Justice - 8.4.4 Child welfare endangerment

8.1.2 Regularisations[72]

Children have the right to conquer free spaces until they come up against sensible limits and rules. They have the right to be democratically involved in all family and care decisions that affect them. The only exception to this is the child's capacity for judgement, which makes participation possible only from a certain level of mental development. Adults must check the capacity for judgement by asking appropriate questions. In case of doubt, the Youth Welfare Office should be consulted. From the age of 10, children receive voting rights for the ministries of family and education. From the age of 18, they have full voting rights for all ministries.

Adults have a duty to establish structures and boundaries in the family or educational institution that are based on benevolent care. Structures are daily routines and rituals in family life or life together. Boundaries are rules that serve to protect others and offer the possibility to accompany children in their boundary crossing. For example, a boundary walk with the child would be to explore the hot cooker top together by carefully approaching the cooker top with your hand and the child's hand to feel when heat becomes uncomfortable and can cause damage. Parents or caregivers have a duty to negotiate boundaries and structures by exchanging arguments with their children. Children should thereby learn assertiveness and develop into responsible citizens. Children are considered assertive when they are taught an understanding of cause and effect and are able to persuade with apt arguments based on the information. Children are considered mature citizens when they follow rules not out of fear of penalty but through understanding. Parents and caregivers therefore have a duty to persevere in explaining and avoiding insufficient boundary setting. Through insufficient boundary setting, children develop unrealistic expectations that ultimately lead to frustration and self-deprecation.

Non-negotiable rules are all laws and other state norms for which the child does not yet have voting rights. Children should learn that they can only negotiate these rules with a majority of many other humans.

72§8,2 Protection of children and youths: BV Art.11

8.1.3 Integrity

Children have the right to physical and mental integrity and safety through balanced nutrition, medical care, rest and exercise without physical punishment and mental injury. They have the right to take risks with their health in order to gain experience through curable injuries and illnesses.
Parents or carers have a duty to provide children with a balanced diet, admission to medical care and sufficient space and time for rest and exercise. They have the right to use their right to determine residence as a punishment and to order the withdrawal of pleasure goods. Punishments must be proportionate and limited in time. Adults must not inflict physical or mental violence on children, such as beatings or verbal abuse. If children themselves first use physical force, they may be detained until they have calmed down. Exceptions apply to the authorities of the Ministry of Security to punish or prevent immediate criminal offences.
Children should thereby develop physical fitness, health resilience, mental steadfastness and healthy self-confidence.
Medical care goes beyond treatments for injuries and illnesses to include vaccinations and screenings for early detection of diseases in children.[73]

8.1.4 Community

Children have the right to stable and supportive communities in the parental home, neighbourhood, peer group or care facility. In these communities, children have a right to age-appropriate, transparent, respectful and friendly handling that prevents exploitation and abuse.
All educational institutions, youth centres and youth organisations are considered care institutions. They have a duty to enable children in their care to form lasting friendships and partnerships as far as possible. Parents have a duty to open up family space by making invitations from peers within and outside their own home the order of the day. Parents and other adults around the child are called upon to create fair,

---

73https://www.bundesgesundheitsministerium.de/u-untersuchung.html

transparent and respectful neighbourly relationships. Adults provide an appropriate environment in which children can get to know each other.

Children should learn to keep friends and partners so that one day they can lead a marriage or be parents themselves. They should develop a sense of justice and solidarity so that they can become responsible nationals.

8.1.5 Talent

Children have the right to have personal experiences in which they can exercise their skills and temperaments to discover their talents. Parents and caregivers have a duty of acceptance and appreciation when the child engages in lawful activities that could not permanently damage his or her health. Children should be able to gain life experiences in order to discover their body's talents and their appeal in life as early as possible.

8.1.6 Experiences

Children have the right to have experiences that are legal for their age. They have the right to form their relationships independently, to solve problems and to fail. Parents and caregivers have a duty to accompany children in this process by giving them advice, support or reassurance. Children should be enabled to master their developmental stages at their own pace. They should receive praise for this in order to be able to feel healthy pride. The Ministry of Family Affairs has the duty to ban violence glorifying impressions for certain age groups and to enact further restrictions through the Youth Protection Act .[74]

8.1.7 Future

Children have the right to a secure future for humanity in a clean environment with a stable ecosystem and a democratically manageable regulatory framework. Adults have the duty to

---

74https://www.gesetze-im-internet.de/juschg/BJNR273000002.html

behave in an exemplary manner towards children and, in the presence of children, also towards adults. Children should develop a sense of democracy and love of country by learning that the world is a structure that can be shaped and not a sinister chaos.

8.2 Children's emergency call

All institutions for the outside care of minors receive a device with a red switch from the Youth Welfare Office. The device must be placed in a place accessible to children. The children must be informed that they should use it as soon as they feel they are being treated unfairly by an adult. As soon as they press the switch, a staff member at the Youth Welfare Office is alerted. The staff member immediately calls the institution, asks the child to tell him what happened and whether he should come by. Next to the device, there is also a telephone number and an intranet address where minors can reach a Youth Welfare Office staff member at any time who will take care of their concerns.

8.3 Child ID[75]

Children receive their child ID card at the Residents' Registration Office after birth.[76] The child ID card is used to process all child benefit bookings. From the age of ten, intranet access and voting rights for the ministries of education and family are activated in the intranet café. A child's parents or their legal representatives are responsible for naming the child. At the age of majority, all citizens have the opportunity to have their first name changed once free of charge. All state services for children are provided immediately after the identity card is expelled.

75§8,2 Protection of children and youths: BV Art.11
76Ministry of Integration - 4.4.1.2 Child ID Card

8.4 Child benefit[77]

The Ministry of Family Affairs is responsible for the amount and payment of child benefits. The amount is measured by the total care expenses of a child who lives in the Social Village full-time throughout the year and resides in the children's home. The necessary data on minimum costs is provided by the ministries of Planned Economy and Education. Since the child benefit is Tax-funded, the people decide on the amount of the child benefit in the coming year in the course of the budget vote.[78] The minimum costs must be covered in order for the children to be able to decide for themselves whether they live with their parents or in the Social Village.

Payment is made by depositing the designated tax funds equally into all children's accounts at People's Bank.[79] The deposit is made at the beginning of a month, of which 1% is directly transferred to the child's pension account. The child benefit can be accessed via the child ID card, which contains the functions of a standard bank card.

Child benefits must primarily be used to pay for services in care facilities where children receive education, exercise, relaxation and meals. The economic form in which the care facility is located or whether the care facility is state-run does not play a role. The remaining balance is only available afterwards. Then any services for the child can be purchased with the amount. This includes food, drinks, clothing, toys, leisure activities, rent, heating, electricity and water. When payment is made, the system automatically checks whether the goods and services are legal for the child and can be used for the child. In the event of a violation, payment is automatically refused. Cash withdrawals are not possible with the bank card for the children's account. Value added tax still applies, but not for state services.

77§234.3 Children's rights, child benefit and parental protection
78Ministry of Finance - 9.5Budget vote
79Ministry of Finance - 11.5.5 Children's account

8.5 Youths

The Ministry of Family Affairs recognises the special needs of youths that they develop, especially from puberty onwards. In this process of detachment from parents, the Ministry of Family Affairs accompanies the youths through Youth Centres and the Youth Alliance. Both institutions offer youths adult reference persons and peer groups. These adult caregivers perform youth social work in the institutions, with which they ensure equal opportunities and integration, as well as providing a minimum of digital equipment.

In particular, youths who are about to reach the age of majority but have not yet finished their school career are supported through voluntary tutoring and mentoring. If necessary, gainful employment is sought with them with which they can pay their living expenses during school education until they have the lowest possible school-leaving qualification. However, this service is not compulsory for youths.

The ministries of family and education provide for cooperation projects between colleges and youth centres or the Youth Alliance. The aim is for college students to act as role models for youths and to be accompanied themselves in their post-puberty.

With its services for youths, the Ministry of Family Affairs ensures that children can be cared for without gaps from the onset of puberty, i.e. from about 10 years of age, until the end of puberty as young adults at up to 30 years of age. In its care, it follows the principle of promoting love and sexuality in order to reduce violence and crime.

8.5.1 Youth Alliance

The Youth Alliance is an organisation of the Ministry of Family Affairs to which children, youths and young adults up to the age of 30 automatically belong. Active membership is voluntary and the pursuit of at least one recreational activity for music, sports, drama or civil defence is funded through child benefits. Adults can participate on an honorary basis, clubs and companies can form partnerships, and state institutions work with the Youth Alliance on an ongoing basis.

The Youth Alliance is an umbrella organisation that offers its own services and can be joined by all clubs, companies and suppliers that offer services for children and youths. Weekly events can be offered by voluntary adults for youths in the youth centres or educational institution. Clubs can also use these institutions and also organise national championships or holiday camps through the Youth Alliance. For example, a gymnastics championship is held with a youth fire brigade camp, so that youths from all over the country arrive as spectators and helpers and are supported.

State institutions are certain authorities of the ministries of security, media, infrastructure and education. The Youth Alliance organises guest lecturers for educational institutions. For example, sports lessons are held by coaches from sports clubs, or teachers from music clubs come for music lessons. The Youth Alliance guarantees state offers for music, sports and drama in every municipality, if necessary, as long as honorary services, clubs or companies do not take over these offers. The state is not allowed to compete with private initiatives. In addition, the Youth Alliance provides youth fire brigades and scouts in every municipality in order to support the authorities for the prevention of danger with young people.[80] It has its own campsites and youth hostels spread throughout the country. There, youths practise cultural exchange and civil defence.

Nationwide youth championships are held annually in the disciplines of music, sports and drama, which the youth fire brigade and the scouts accompany with a tent camp by providing accommodation and food. The Youth Alliance organises the events in cooperation with disaster management[81] and Youth Television[82] . These events encourage youths to exchange experiences, to get out of their local situation and to make new acquaintances throughout the country through major supra-regional events. Continent-wide and worldwide events are organised in cooperation with the Ministry of

---

80 Ministry of Security - 5 Prevention of danger
81 Ministry of Security - 5.7 Disaster management
82 Ministry of Media - 14 Youth Television

Foreign Affairs.

8.5.1.1 Youth Fire Brigade

The youth fire brigade trains in rescue from fire, water, ice, stone, plastic and metal as well as first aid to humans. The youth fire brigade is organised on a municipal level and supports the fire brigade with non-hazardous services during operations. Disaster management is organised nationally. All youth fire brigades in the country are invited to participate in large-scale exercises. Additional instruction forces are then available for large-scale operations.

8.5.1.2 Scouts

The scouts practise living in the field. They know how to orientate themselves in nature, hunt, gather and prepare food, build shelters and start fires. The highlight is the annual camp season. Each camp lasts one week. First there are many small municipal camps that take place in the wild nature. Then there are larger camps on campgrounds in which many municipalities participate. At the end, there are tent camps for participants from all over the inland at the Youth Alliance's largest campsites, in which the local youth fire brigade also participates and national championships are held for music, sports and drama.

8.5.1.3 Disaster management

The youth fire brigade organises exercises in cooperation with disaster management, which are also used to hold regional championships in music, sports and drama. The exercises last 3 to 4 days and take place on extended weekends. On leap years, there is a large-scale exercise in summer that lasts a week and is supported by the scouts with tents. What is practised is the evacuation of the population in container buildings and the fight against a disaster. The participants of the championships are the extras of the exercise, which are equipped by the actors and staged in voting with the exercise leaders. The members of the youth fire brigade practise on the extras and provide accommodation and food.

8.5.2 Youth centre

Young humans want to test their limits during puberty and get to know and love the opposite sex. For this, the youth centres offer them the basic conditions which they can use for themselves through their own initiative. The Youth Welfare Office runs youth centres in all municipalities. Each youth centre consists of a central office and a varying number of branches. The size of the head office and the number of branches depends on the number of youths and young adults in a municipality who want to use the youth centre.

Conflicts are resolved according to the education court method,[83] or mediation cells are ordered from the Ministry of Security. In addition, at the request of the youths affected, mediation cells can be set up in cooperation with the police and under the supervision of the People's Protection Service, and duels and brawls can be organised as long as enough participants can be found. Duels may only be held in the youth centre without the use of weapons and equal protective equipment.[84] The reduction of aggression and violent fantasies is promoted through martial arts and drama.

If drug use by minors is detected, the police are informed. The People's Protection Service regularly visits the youth centres and branches and inquires about the general well-being. In case of suspicion of drug abuse or possession of weapons, a search of persons may be carried out.

8.5.2.1 Head office

The head office is a building with rooms such as a parent-child room, bedroom, study room, office, bathroom, toilet, kitchen, bar, living room, playroom and workshop. Workers

---

83 Ministry of Education - 5.10.7 Education court
84 Ministry of Security - 6.6 Dispute Resolution, 7 Police, 6 People's Protection Service

from the Youth Welfare Office work in cooperation with youths to design, furnish and sustainably manage the premises according to their majority wishes. The centre serves as a residential community with constantly changing residents. The aim is to give youths and young adults the opportunity to live away from their parents' home for a while.

Youths parents are given the opportunity to remain members of their peer group despite having their own children. Especially for this target group, there is a parent-child room where a cradle, cot and changing table are available.

On the one hand, the bedroom serves as a place to sleep for teenage runaways or sleeping accommodation for tired youths. On the other hand, it also serves as a co-bedroom where youths and young adults can have sex. Contraceptives are available. Should one sexual partner become uncomfortable and the other sexual partner does not leave even after being asked to do so, a call for help is sufficient. Therefore, the room is not lockable. Only a door sign indicates whether the room is occupied or free.

The study room is open to all youths and young adults who want to further their education. Here, older youths can tutor younger youths, form study groups or work on their own. The study room has all the latest digital learning tools from the People's Innovation Company[85] intranet.[86]

Youth Welfare Office workers have their workplace in the office, where youths can also work when it comes to the youth centre's housekeeping. For accounting and housekeeping services, the youths divide themselves digitally.[87]

The bathroom has a shower, bathtub, toilet and 2 washbasins, the WC has 2 toilets and 2 washbasins. The kitchen contains all the essential kitchen appliances, such as a hob, fridge, dryer and washing machine, as well as the necessary cutlery.

The bar has a counter, tables and chairs where people eat, drink, talk and play. The living room has sofas, a DJ booth and a dance floor or stage. In the playroom, youths have the opportunity to play the games of their age group and to acquire

---

85Ministry of Innovation - 10 People's Innovation Company
86Ministry of Digital Affairs - 13 People's Innovation Company Intranet
87Ministry of Planned Economy - 7.6.1 Digital duty roster

more toys by donating, repairing or building their own. The workshop is used to build and repair items, especially for construction work at the branches. The workshop has several sets of tools that are lent out to the branches and machines that are used to make work pieces that are destined for the branches or the head office.

8.5.2.2 Branches

The branches are premises that the youths build and manage themselves in a responsible and democratic way. If they need help, they can ask for it from the staff at the head office. The Youth Welfare Office staff is responsible for technical issues, and they receive technical support from the Building Office[88]
. Simplified building regulations apply. All existing branches must be used first before new ones may be developed. If a group of youths wants to occupy an existing branch or start a new branch, they have to apply for it at the youth centre. There it is checked whether the branches are already used to capacity or whether there is a vacancy. Existing branches are passed on from generation to generation by the youths of a municipality. For new branches, the youths have to name the desired locations when applying. The Youth Welfare Office asks the Building Office for the location. If the Building Office rejects the location, it designates a location that is within about 2 kilometres of the youths' homes.
Each youth centre is given a plot of land as a branch in the nearest state forest, where youths are allowed to build wooden huts or tree houses to live out their home-building instinct. In the forest, the use of plastics that cannot decompose is prohibited. This applies to both construction and use. The only exception is glass, which may be used for construction. Mobile dwellings may be used in urban areas and peripheral areas of state forests. These mobile dwellings are provided by the Ministry of Infrastructure and consist of disused construction trucks, containers, train carriages, aeroplanes or buses. The youths can extend and convert them as they wish, as long as they democratically agree on it.

88Ministry of Infrastructure - 5.1 Building Office

Branches must not cause litter or noise nuisance. For this, the youths who have registered a branch must set up a rubbish service that collects surrounding rubbish and disposes of it properly. Those who litter youth centres will receive additional litter service as a sentence and will be banned from using the branch for 6 months if they receive 3 sentences in 12 months. A noise traffic light will be placed on the first complaint of noise nuisance. If littering or noise nuisance still occurs, the branch will be closed for 3 months or handed over to another group of youths. Branches are visited daily by Youth Welfare Office staff to check on child welfare, litter and noise nuisance, as well as to educate youths about sexuality and drugs, or to resolve conflicts.

8.6 Youth protection laws

The minors are informed annually about their rights and obligations arising from the laws on the protection of children and young people. On the one hand, this includes the duties, at what age they are allowed to move around for how long alone in public, become legally competent or are allowed to buy and consume drugs. On the other hand, the rights to the best interests of the child are explained and what obligations arise from this for parents, teachers, other adults and children. The Ministry of Family Affairs, in voting with the Ministry of Health, imposes restrictions on the use of things that cause permanent damage to the mental or physical development of adolescents up to a certain age.

Minors up to the age of 10 are allowed to stay unaccompanied in public until 10 pm. Up to the age of 18, the same applies until midnight. Raw meat and the use of screens and the intranet are permitted for children from the age of 6. Internet use is allowed from the age of 10. Drugs, including caffeine and violent media content and behaviour, are permitted from the age of 18.

Age restrictions are checked at the time of sale or consumption. Those who do not know the age of adolescents must have their identity card shown. Those who know the age shall keep age-restricted items inaccessible and set up separate admissions with separate passwords on devices that are internet or intranet enabled. The rights of use for the child's admission should be restricted according to the child's age. Suppliers of age-restricted content or products are required to provide the simplest possible user separation, which must be checked by the Company Auditing Agency before approval.

8.7 Age of majority

The age of majority is determined by the people in a voting. The age of majority is reached on the 18th birthday. From this point onwards, age restrictions no longer apply and those entitled to vote are fully entitled to vote, to commit criminal offences and to be legally competent. Even before the age of majority, driving a motor vehicle on the road is permitted from the age of 14, as long as it does not exceed the maximum speed of 40km/h. At the age of 16, the maximum speed is increased to 80km/h. Already from the age of 10, the age of criminal responsibility exists, which is restricted until the age of majority. The restriction lies in the liability for costs in the event of damage, which must be borne by the parents, and in the level of punishment, which is divided between underage offenders and their parents. From the age of 14, youths have limited legal capacity. Their weekly working hours may not exceed 12 hours as long as they are of compulsory school age and have no educational qualifications. They may not enter into treaties for loans and subscriptions unless they have an educational qualification and are running a company. Voting rights for the ministries of education and family are granted to nationals from the age of 10.

9 Leisure[89]

The Ministry of Family Affairs is responsible for ensuring that citizens have a variety of opportunities to care for their culture in their free time. State funding is provided by the Ministry of Family Affairs for music, arts and sports. In this context, the Youth Welfare Office, the Youth Alliance and Seniors' Alliance

---

89 §184,4,5 Promotion of music, sport, film, culture and art: BV

work with clubs that are open to all age groups, as well as with other ministries. The Ministries of Education, Media, Health and Infrastructure support the Ministry of Family Affairs in providing state services for music, arts and sports.

The prerequisite for the state operation of museums, theatres and concert halls is the economic viability of the enterprises, which the Ministry of Family Affairs operates with a profit margin of 10%. Subsidies from tax funds are not permitted.

9.1 Art[90]

The visual and performing arts form the two categories for art. The concept of art itself is free and is legally limited only by the constitution. Artistic crafts can be practised in workshops of educational institutions or youth centres, no matter how old the artists are. Which state spaces are made available to artists is determined by the ministries for family and infrastructure in voting with each other.

The Ministry of Family Affairs promotes the visual arts through exhibitions in public spaces. Facades of state buildings can be covered with graffiti or paintings free of charge and for a limited period of time, and canvases and sculptures are set up on traffic islands. Revenues for artists in public spaces come from donations. On publicly accessible artworks, artists are allowed to indicate the bank details to their donation account. Companies of any economic form may operate museums.

The Ministry of Family Affairs promotes the performing arts through events in public spaces. Performing drama and dance can be performed in squares and town halls free of charge and for a limited period of time. Performers may designate an audience area for which they may charge admission fees. Companies of any economic form may operate theatres, opera houses and cinema halls. The Ministry of Media Affairs supports the performing arts by providing free use of the People's Motor Vehicle[91] as a stage following state events.

Art.67a, 68, 69, 71
90 §19 Freedom of art
91 Ministry of Media - 7.1.1 People's Motor Vehicle

9.2 Music[92]

The Ministry of Family Affairs promotes musicians through the free and time-limited use of public space. Musicians are allowed to place themselves on streets and squares between 6 a.m. and 10 p.m. and play music there for a maximum of 60 minutes. After the time has expired, they must move to another place that is no longer within earshot. The same place may not be used again until the following day. Electronic or acoustic instruments may be electronically amplified up to 80 decibels. Musicians may set up containers for donations and sell their specially composed music on recordings. Companies of any economic form may operate music schools, operas and concert halls.

The Ministry of Education promotes music through music classes in educational institutions open to all age groups. The Ministry of Media Affairs supports musicians through the free use of the People's Motor Vehicle as a stage following state events.

9.3 Sport[93]

The Ministries of Infrastructure and Health provide sports facilities for general fitness.[94] The Ministry of Education provides physical education and the Ministry of Social Market Economy provides company sports.[95] The Ministry of Family Affairs is responsible for making all sports facilities accessible to citizens of all ages and ensures the necessary cooperation with sports clubs. The aim is to have as few unused sports facilities as possible.

The Ministry of Family Affairs, in voting with the other ministries, provides sufficient sports facilities in the municipalities. These include swimming pools, fitness trails and sports fields for ball games and athletics that can be used

---

92§184.1 Promotion of music, sport, film, culture and art: BV Art.67a
93§184.2 Promotion of music, sport, film, culture and art: BV Art.68
94Ministry of Health - 6.2 Exercise, Ministry of Infrastructure - 4.6 Leisure
95Ministry of Education - 8.7.4.8 Sport, 9.15.2.3 Sport, Ministry of Social Market Economy - 6.10 Company Sport

in different ways. In housing estates, sufficient climbing trees must be planted to provide natural training for the back and shoulder muscles free of charge for young and old.

Sports clubs and citizens interested in sports have the possibility to use sports facilities of the Ministry of Education while no classes are being held there. Learners and teachers of the affected educational institution have first right of access in case of shortage.

The Ministry of Family Affairs is responsible for elite sport. It maintains sports facilities in its capital city to promote elite sport and to send athletes from all clubs in the country to world championships and the Olympics. Clubs with the same sports are automatically members of the respective sports federation. Clubs identify their most successful members in competitions and report them to the sports federation, which in turn reports the country's most successful athletes to the Ministry of Family Affairs. The health auditors of the Company Auditing Agency[96] ensure the national and international fight against doping and the legality auditors ensure the integrity and values in sport for fairness and caring training methods.

9.4 Recreational events

The Ministry of Family Affairs supports independently organised recreational events by citizens with a fund of equipment to run events. This fundus is a database of all items in storage facilities in the municipality that contain toys and event equipment. This includes a stage, lighting equipment, tables and benches, radio transmitters for the local area and toys from the playgrounds' cupboards.

For example, to organise a city dance without disturbing the peace, the radio station can be lent out and all participants with radio receivers and headphones can listen to the sounds that a band or DJ feeds into the mobile radio station.

96Ministry of Labour - 20.7.2 Health auditor

9.5 Playgrounds

The Ministry of Family Affairs, in voting with the Ministry of Infrastructure, ensures the construction and operation of playgrounds as recreational centres for all age groups. The Ministry of Family Affairs decides on the type of playgrounds at the respective locations. It is guided by the age structure and the expressed needs of the local population. It also ensures that the playgrounds are equipped with toys. The Ministry of Infrastructure is responsible for the construction and operation of recreation centres as well as the operation of other institutions and events for recreation.[97] Residents can report suggestions and complaints via the Ministry of Family Affairs' intranet page in the State Directory. Clubs can apply for the use of playgrounds in the Club Directory.

Playgrounds are mandatory in urban areas to promote children's movement development that would otherwise have been facilitated in outdoor movement games. Playgrounds are found in residential areas and are part of every Leisure Centre. Playgrounds with recreation centres also have recreation rooms with changing rooms and sanitary facilities. Standardised containers are used as recreation rooms, or disused construction trailers, living containers, wagons, ships or aeroplanes, depending on the size of the Leisure Centre.

9.5.1 Toy cupboard

Each playground has a cupboard with toys. Volunteers can donate worn-out toys there. Youth Welfare Office staff regularly control the cupboards for completeness, replace broken toys and ensure a balanced distribution of toys in all toy cupboards in the municipality.

Depending on the type and environment of the playground, there are suitable toys in the cupboard. These are, for example, experimental kits for acoustics, biology, chemistry, electronics, optics, mechanics, computer science, musical instruments, props, sand toys, slips of paper and pens. All toys are locked in the cupboard. Anyone who opens the locker door with their

---

97 Ministry of Infrastructure - 4.6 Leisure

identity card is responsible for the material. Damage must be reported immediately. The cupboard is specially equipped for this.

To operate the cabinet, a computer in the form of a touch screen (tablet PC) with light, camera and microphone is permanently installed on the inside of each of the right and left doors on a vertically adjustable carriage device. This allows humans of different heights to use the cabinet. In addition, the Tablet PCs can be used as a height-adjustable and swivelling light source. The cameras of the Tablet PCs form a photo box when the doors are open.

The lock on the cupboard door is a card reader that can only be opened with an identity card. To do this, the identity card must be fully inserted. The identity card is only reissued when the return has been successfully completed and the results of all scales are correct. There are scales in the shelves of the cupboard. Each toy has a specific weight and must be returned to the shelves in the same compartment. If the weighed weight changes, the identity card will not be expelled. If not all the weights have been weighed as saved, the incorrect toy must be scanned individually by barcode and then placed in the appropriate compartment to be weighed. If a wrong result is still displayed, the toy must be photographed in the photo box. If a part is defective, it will also be placed in the photo box so that the damage can be documented. The photo box is only big enough to fit each toy individually. You can take photos as often as you like until you have taken the right shot. As soon as you select the shot, you have to scan the barcode of the toy that is broken. The maintenance service will replace the toy during the regular visit. Anyone who loses toys or has them stolen must indicate this in the tablet PC and the goods will be replaced. The invoice is sent to the address expelled in the identity card.

9.5.2 Noise traffic light

A decibel meter with microphone, warning lights, loudspeaker and camera is set up at each playground or youth centre if more than 3 residents per year complain to the police about noise nuisance. The measuring system has a readable clock and thus recognises when night silence is called for. A built-in microphone measures the volume and displays it on an LED panel next to the clock. A green light lights up when the volume does not exceed 50 decibels (dB) during the day between 6 am and 10 pm and 30dB at night.[98] Between 10am and 8pm, the noise level may be up to 80db. A yellow light flashes when the limit range is reached in 10dB and a red light is lit when the limit range is exceeded. When the red light is on, the microphone records the sound and after 20 minutes of continued exceeding, the police are alerted. They can then see and hear what is going on with the surveillance camera and microphone and make announcements over the loudspeaker. If the violations are too frequent, the playground or the youth centre branch will be temporarily closed. The power supply can also be temporarily throttled automatically.

9.6 Clubs[99]

Citizens have the right to form clubs in order to implement joint projects in a targeted manner. The Ministry of Family Affairs regulates the requirements for clubs in the law on clubs. The Company Auditing Agency audits whether and how the clubs comply with the requirements every 3 years.

Clubs are regular gatherings of voluntary members geared to a defined purpose. They do not seek to make a profit and use their revenues only to fulfil the defined purpose. Clubs that wish to make profits must be registered as companies in the appropriate economic form. Unlike Non-profit companies, their members do the work and are also customers of that work.

Citizens report the unification in the Club Directory. To disclose their purpose, members describe their intentions in the club's statutes. Each club must publish its statutes in the Law Directory and may edit them there with digital amendment

---

98https://www.juraforum.de/lexikon/ruhestoerung#ruhestoerung-ab-wann-erlaubte-immissionsrichtwerte-in-dezibel-db-als-zimmerlautstaerke
99§21 Freedom of Association: BV Art.23

measures in voting with all members.[100] The contents of club's statutes must not contradict the constitution and the laws. This is ensured by an automated comparison of the statutes with all other entries in the Law Directory. The members of the club elect a leader, deputy leader and treasurer.

9.6.1 Club Directory

With the Club Directory, all citizens have the opportunity to use their freedom of unification and find humans with matching interests or skills. In the Club Directory, all unifications have a profile. There they list all their services and events. Users who follow the profiles are members of the club. They are listed in a database on the club's profile and their activity in the club is noted. Honorary service organisations that are organised as a club also receive a profile. Honorary service providers who offer their service alone or in an alliance of a maximum of 3 persons can also create a profile and do not have to found a club.

Clubs that offer services or events together with other clubs or are involved in a specific project can set up a group. The group function can be used for agreements, voting and the distribution of tasks.

9.7 Honorary service

Honorary service is characterised by voluntary Non-profit work that is remunerated at most with an expense allowance. Honorary service can be created and performed by citizens on a voluntary basis. The Ministry of Education maintains the People's Service as a compulsory period during which honorary services can be undertaken for a maximum of 6 months. In order to promote private honorary service, the Ministry of Family Affairs maintains an Engagement Foundation that promotes honorary service by assessing eligibility and disbursing grant funds or forwarding in-kind donations to appropriate honorary organisations. Honorary services must

---

100 Ministry of Justice - 4.7 Law Directory

be registered as a club or company. A temporary honorary service or one carried out by a maximum of 3 persons for the sake of charity does not need to be registered.

10 Senior citizens

The Ministry of Family Affairs accompanies senior citizens from retirement age until death. The accompaniment serves to ensure that senior citizens can live self-determined lives for as long as possible and receive all the pension and care benefits to which they are entitled. The Ministry of Health regulates the financing and executive of care for the elderly.[101] The Ministry of Labour, in voting with the Ministries of Economy and Finance, regulates the financing and payment of the pension.[102]

The Ministry of Family Affairs organises cooperation between senior citizens and educational institutions or companies. Senior citizens can visit educational institutions to supervise minors or to attend classes. Senior citizens are only allowed to attend classes if there are enough free places and teachers. Senior citizens can continue to be gainfully employed. Companies that cannot find skilled workers can send news to all senior citizens who have the appropriate qualifications. Companies do not get admission to the data, but send their search request together with the job advertisement to the Labour Directory. Using the archived data from the Education Directory and Labour Directory of the senior citizen, matching senior citizens in the vicinity are displayed. Companies see the number of suitably qualified senior citizens and can extend the radius if the number is too small.

10.1 Seniors' Alliance

The Seniors' Alliance takes over the communication between responsible bodies for the accommodation, care and support of senior citizens. Every person of retirement age is automatically a member of the Seniors' Alliance. Members

---

101 Ministry of Health - 5.7 Care
102 Ministry of Labour - 21 Pension

can find admission to benefits and other senior citizens with the same interests more easily with the help of the Seniors' Alliance.

Through the Family, Real Estate and Care Directories, multi-generational homes, senior living communities and honourary and professional care are supported. To better connect senior citizens, the Family Directory has the senior citizens group. It has subgroups for residential homes, meetings, outings and unmated or widowed senior citizens. The Seniors' Alliance regularly organises housing inspections, partner exchanges, outings, dances and games meetings. It represents the interests of senior citizens vis-à-vis the Ministry of Family Affairs.

10.2 Retirement home

While Residential Communities of senior citizens only share rent and outpatient care workers, senior citizens can also be accommodated in cooperative retirement homes. The Ministry of Family Affairs runs such retirement homes if enough senior citizens pay enough entrance fees to finance the construction. The owners of these old people's homes are the senior citizens who are currently living in them. They are democratically involved in all planning measures. When they move out or pass away, they get the entrance fee back. The construction and operation is administered by the Ministry of Family Affairs in cooperation with the Ministries of Infrastructure and Health. Senior citizens who live in it pay a monthly contribution to cover the costs of staff and materials. The costs for construction and operation are covered by the interest income from the invested entrance fees and contributions and include a 10% profit mark-up.

11 Death[103]

The Ministry of Family Affairs is responsible for making death as part of life as pleasant as possible for all participants. The basic principle is that every human being owns his or her life and may decide to end it at any time. In order to make death as harmless as possible for fellow human beings and relatives, death by suicide or illness that can be planned is introduced with measures and requirements. Measures are medical treatments that lead to a painless death and requirements are testaments or inheritance contracts.

As soon as a person dies, a physician must determine the death and issue a death certificate. The Registry Office is responsible for issuing the death certificate, with which all memberships of the deceased can be terminated immediately and a funeral can be organised. The relatives can take care of this or have it done by the Registry Office for a fee. Bereaved relatives can be assisted by the cure of souls. Persons who need personal support because they are in deep mourning can move into the Social Village Hotel for a short time or into the Social Village for a longer period.

If the deceased has no relatives, the Registry Office will take care of the termination of all memberships and treaties. The Social Service takes care of the funeral.[104] It covers its costs as far as possible from the estate.

11.1 Inheritance

The Ministry of Family Affairs is responsible for legislation on inheritance law. Inheritance law covers the handling of the estate of a deceased person, the So-called testator. The estate consists of the assets, i.e. any property and alienable rights of the deceased. The law of succession regulates the transfer of assets from the deceased to one or more other persons, the So-called heirs.

The succession is regulated by law through a standardised testament, which the testator can amend at the Registry Office according to his or her own ideas through the So-called

---

103§4.1 Right to life: BV Art.10
104Ministry of Planned Economy - 6.5 Death

freedom to make a will. He can also make changes to the lawful testament in an inheritance contract with persons chosen by him. While the testament can only be revoked by the testator at any time, the revocation or amendment of an inheritance contract is only possible with the consent of all contracting parties.

11.1.1 Testament

The testator can amend the testament at any time and must have the currently valid original kept at the Registry Office. In particular, he or she can disinherit certain persons, change the order of succession and distribute the compulsory portions differently. Via the People's Computer, every citizen can access his or her digital testament, which is stored in a database of the Registry Office on the intranet. The database can be accessed via the profile page of the Ministry of Family Affairs in the State Directory. Users can only view and edit their own wills at a time. Alternatively, citizens can file their wills in person at the Registry Office in paper form. The Registry Office checks the submitted testament to see if it meets all the requirements of the law, scans it and uploads it to the database. In this way, the reading of the will can take place in any Registry Office without the inheritors having to meet for this purpose in a Registry Office.

11.1.1.1 Personal data

All persons, including the author of the testament must be named with their first and last names, date of birth and place of birth. Wills in paper form must be handwritten and bear the person's own signature. Digital wills must be written on the person's own People's Computer and uploaded to the Registry Office database. A voice sample must be submitted for confirmation, which is checked for each digital change.

11.1.1.2 Succession

Legal succession is based on the degree of kinship. Closer relatives are entitled to inherit before distant relatives. This means that the spouse or spouses come first, followed by one's own children, one's own parents and finally one's own siblings.

11.1.1.3 Compulsory part

The compulsory portion is measured by the amount of the inheritance, the number of heirs and the degree of relationship. It applies to spouses, ancestors and descendants. If there are up to 2 children, each child receives 20%; if there are 3 or more children, 60% of the inheritance is distributed equally to all children. Parents each receive 12.5% of the inheritance if they are still alive. The rest of the inheritance goes to surviving spouses. If a testator no longer has any living relatives, no spouse or children and has not distributed his or her inheritance, the inheritance flows equally to all generation accounts at People's Bank.[105]

11.2 Suicide

Suicide is in principle legal. Other persons may perform euthanasia, the procedure for which is laid down in a contract to kill. All persons providing euthanasia and the person willing to die must individually declare their consent at the Registry Office and sign the contract to kill. Persons willing to die who do not wish to use persons for euthanasia can visit suicide cells.

The suicide cells are operated at cemeteries with crematoria. A physician is present at the appointed time. To commit suicide, one has to call the Registry Office or fill out a form on the intranet site of the Ministry of Family Affairs. You are then given three appointments until you die. At the first appointment, you talk to psychologists and social workers who encourage you to live and show you ways out of comparable cases. At the second appointment, the inheritance and the

---

105 Ministry of Finance - 11.5.7 Generation Account

funeral arrangements are discussed with lawyers, registrars and funeral directors. The third appointment is in the suicide cell. For the last time, the physician who will diagnose the death and fill out the death certificate will ask you if you really want to die. If the answer is yes, the physician hands out the pills that will make the suicide fall asleep. The physician closes the door behind the suicide to ensure that the tablets are not stolen. Now you undress, pack your clothes and everything still on your body into a rubbish bag, lie down on the couch and swallow the tablets with tap water. There is a heart rate monitor in the couch that is connected to the physician. As soon as it no longer measures a pulse, the physician is notified. The physician goes to the deceased and checks the heart, breath and iris and declares the dying person dead. Afterwards, one is driven out of the suicide cell on the stretcher past the waiting suicides to the crematorium. The suicides are to see what fate will soon befall them. The urn with the ashes can now be picked up by relatives or is disposed of in the organic waste. As a voluntary donation, hair is shorn for wigs or blood and organs are collected. In the case of blood and organ removal, the suicide takes place in the hospital according to the same procedure. The killing is done with means that do not damage the organs, or the blood, but are as short and painless as the pills in the suicide cell.

11.3 Burial

In principle, any form of burial that the deceased has wished for in the testament is permitted. The only restriction is that no one may be harmed in the process. Municipal cemeteries may decide independently which forms of burial they offer. For reasons of space, cities may prescribe the reburial of graves after 100 years, even if they are urn graves. Cemeteries are either run by the Municipal Utilities Company[106] or by private and church organisations. Burying the ashes from an urn in a place of one's own choosing or disposing of them in the wind or water is permissible, provided the deceased has stipulated it in the testament.

106 Ministry of Infrastructure - 4.9 Municipal Utilities Company

11.4 Ancestral Archive

Every descendant can research his or her ancestors in the ancestral archive. All documents of the past are photographed or scanned in order to be able to access the ancestral archive as completely as possible digitally via the intranet. As of digital citizen registration in directories and People's Computers for the intranet, descendants have access to the profiles of all their ancestors' directories. Of course, they can no longer edit them, but only read them.

12 Switching to the new system

The Ministry of Family Affairs is redistributing and centralising the tasks of the registry and Youth Welfare Offices. This means that all offices in the municipalities work in a national alliance and exchange data. The Ministry of Family Affairs needs the responsibility from the municipalities and the regions for this.

12.1 Conversion of the foundations

The state foundations for honorary service are transformed into the Engagement Foundation. Military service is transferred to the People's Service and youth volunteering is taken over by the Youth Alliance.

The foundations for Contergan victims, children in care as well as the sexual abuse fund are dissolved on a cut-off date and the amounts are paid out to those affected who have reported by the cut-off date.

12.2 Amendment of the Sexual Offences Act

The criminal law on sexual offences is amended so that it is no longer sex that is punishable, but coercion, harassment, blackmail, kidnapping, human trafficking, bodily harm, murder or other offences without a sexual background. The punishable acts and the sexual handling of and with minors are changed according to the new regularisations.

12.3 Conversion of cultural funding

State museums are privatised and all art objects are sold to the highest bidder. Looted art is returned. Objects of art that the majority of the population determines to be their cultural property may not be sold, but only rented out with the obligation to exhibit them in museums in the country. The money generated flows into the state cultural institutions for music, art and sport. The promotion of elite sport is discontinued in favour of mass sport and continues exclusively in the performance centre in the capital city of the Ministry of Family Affairs.

12.4 Introduction of the parenting licence

The parenting licence will be introduced as soon as possible. All parents who find out about their pregnancy from the cut-off date will take the parenting licence, other parents can take it voluntarily. For this purpose, the vocational training colleges for social education prepare the appropriate curriculum in cooperation with the subject areas for education at the vocational training colleges and universities. The nursery schools, primary schools and secondary schools provide the facilities outside regular opening hours. The teaching and support staff of these institutions provide lessons for the parenting licence.

12.5 Conversion of the old ministries

For the conversion of the old ministries, all departments and units of the old ministries that are changing to this ministry are identified. The organigrams are used to determine whether an entire department and all its units are changing or only individual units. All unsuitable departments and units are dropped. The existing staff adapts its tasks to the new requirements.

Contact form

Dear reader
If you would like to make what you have read come true, in whole or in part, together with other like-minded people, I offer you several possibilities with this contact form. Fill it out, tear out the page and send it by post to:
Andreas Seidl, P.O. Box 1206, 63488 Seligenstadt / Germany

Or send the details to:
Phone: 0049 1522 818 2243 (whatsapp, telegram, signal)
Email: andreas.seidl2022@web.de

Please mark with a cross:
O   I want to found a dynamic People's Party.
O   I want to donate money for implementation.
O   I want contacts with like-minded people in my area.

Forename: ____

Surname: ____

Please fill in only the contact option through which a reply should be made.

Street, house no.:   ____________________________________

Postcode, city, country: ____________________________________

Phone: ____________________________________

Email address: ____________________________________